T0289774

World of Workcraft

For those that are nesh.

Those shivers are not born of thin skin, physical weakness, a wiry frame or poor clothing. They are genuine. Life's cold blast can chill them to the bone. They feel the warmth deeply too. Their gift and curse is to be able to deal with infinite variation, the subtlest nuance, and distinguish a thousand shades of grey where others only see black and white. Their perceptions are finely attuned to the universe around them. Here's to the nesh, the world would not change without them.

World of Workcraft

Rediscovering Motivation and
Engagement in the
Digital Workplace

DALE ROBERTS

GOWER

Published by
Gower Publishing Limited
Wey Court East
Union Road
Farnham
Surrey, GU9 7PT
England

Gower Publishing Company
110 Cherry Street
Suite 3-1
Burlington, VT 05401-3818
USA

www.gowerpublishing.com

British Library Cataloguing in Publication Data
A catalogue record for this book is available from the British Library.

Library of Congress Cataloging-in-Publication Data
Roberts, Dale, 1963–
    World of workcraft : rediscovering motivation and engagement in the digital workplace / by Dale Roberts.
        pages cm
    Includes bibliographical references and index.
    ISBN 978-1-4724-2905-6 (hardback : alk. paper) – ISBN 978-1-4724-2906-3 (ebook) – ISBN 978-1-4724-2907-0 (epub)
    1. Employee motivation. 2. Games – Psychological aspects. 3. Organizational behavior.
I. Title.
    HF5549.5.M63R624 2015
    658.3'14015193 – dc23

                                                        2014049877

ISBN: 9781472429056 (hbk)
ISBN: 9781472429063 (ebk – ePDF)
ISBN: 9781472429070 (ebk – ePUB)

Printed in the United Kingdom by Henry Ling Limited, at the Dorset Press, Dorchester, DT1 1HD

Contents

List of Figures and Tables

Figures

Tables

Foreword

TOBY BERESFORD

When the editors of *Encyclopædia Britannica*, with its two hundred year history, looked at Wikipedia in 2009 they dismissed it as 'fun'.[1] Becoming a contributor and tracking your progress is surely not enough to motivate serious researchers and writers? Yet only three years later they closed the door of the printing press on their last ever print edition.

When Mark Zuckerberg wanted to reach a billion people with his social network, Facebook, he added a 'like' button so we could get instant, quantified feedback from those closest to us on what we say and do. By 2013 we were 'liking' each other's content over 4.5 billion times a day.[2]

Both organisations have successfully taken the power of games and applied their principles to the world of business.

This application of game thinking, known as 'gamification', is really 'player-led design' – it's redesigning what your organisation does but from the perspective of the player whether they are an employee or a customer.

Player-led designers ask questions like 'if I was "playing" at being an encyclopædia entry writer – what feedback would I want?' or 'if I was "playing" at sharing my life with friends, what feedback would I want?'

The right answers to these questions lead to new, hyper-engaging and super-valuable products and services.

In this well-timed book, Dale Roberts delightfully takes us on a journey through the most important applications, people and concepts that you'll need to understand and then apply the power of 'gamification' to your own organisation. His no-nonsense, straightforward style, dodges the hyperbole that new technologies often bring with them. Instead he gives us real, proven

---

1   https://en.wikipedia.org/wiki/Encyclop%C3%A6dia_Britannica.
2   https://zephoria.com/social-media/top-15-valuable-facebook-statistics/.

and applicable examples of how real organisations like yours and mine are seeing their competitors fade into the distance in their rear view mirrors.

In Part I, he improves his fitness by running from zombies and playing piano on the stairs. Then he shows us how our understanding of how money motivates us is wrong. He describes how to get our fence painted by persuading our friends to pay for the experience and how paying someone more, can sometimes mean you get worse performance, than if you paid them less.

In Part II, Roberts neatly summarises the modern motivational thinking of leading behavioural economists such as the two Dans (Pink and Ariely). The way we motivate our staff and customers has changed, to win we must understand this new approach.

Finally, in Part III, we are given a treasure map for our own gamification journey. While I can't promise that X will mark the spot for your particular pot of gold, you can certainly set out, confident that you are in the hands of a master navigator.

Toby Beresford is CEO and founder of Rise.global, a gamified performance tracking tool used by global businesses to encourage staff with personal feedback and peer recognition alone. He is founder of the London Gamifiers meetup and the founding chair of GamFed the international gamification confederation. He is a popular public speaker and publishes the worldwide 'Gamification Gurus Power 100 Leaderboard', one of the world's first successful infinite gamification programs, helping spread awareness of gamification via digital media.

Preface

The air is thick with cold mist as I make last-minute preparations for an early-morning run. The muscles in my legs are barely awake as I try and shake some life into them whilst simultaneously generating just enough body heat to encourage me to unfold my arms, currently involuntarily wrapped around my upper body for warmth. After shivering through neck rolls, high knee kicks and arm stretches, but still feeling anything other than warmed up, I set off. That initial uncertain, clumsy gait as I plod down the hill is more a product of setting off out of a sense of time passing than any state of readiness. Ready, I'm not.

The road circles around, ending in a cul-de-sac, and then becomes a footpath around a small lake. Even at this early hour there's a man fishing, sitting in quiet determination, contemplating his chances of a catch in return for his patience. A young woman, perhaps his partner, sits nearby, smoking and staring at exactly the same point in the water as her angling companion.

My pace increases as I skirt around one edge of the lake, through a gate and onto the canal path. I can feel the sting of cold on my legs, not yet warm from exertion, and it coaxes an unconscious increase in pace. I can feel my own icy breath as I inhale, and I jealously cling on to exhalation as if it were a warm blanket and relinquishing it would result in an unwelcome drop in body temperature.

A voice in my ear describes a small camp just a few hundred metres away. The people there, apparently, are self-sufficient, with ample food and medical supplies. It's an early-morning run, I'm only a couple of kilometres in, and have reached a secluded part of the canal tow path that I'm fortunate to have as my regular running route. The voice goes on. The settlers in the camp are also well armed. This turns out to be a good thing for them, because the area is surrounded by zombies.

This is no ordinary run. I am Runner 5, tasked with investigating the origins of the zombie outbreak and finding Patient Zero. In a world succumbing to the undead, runners are needed for communications and to perform the occasional daring rescue. When the world is in short supply of oil but all stocked up on walking corpses, being fast on your feet becomes currency.

The next transmission is interrupted, and I am alerted to a zombie a few metres away and closing in behind me – 60 metres, then 50 ... beep, 25 ... beep beep, 10 ... beep beep beep. Now I can hear inhuman grunting and growling, getting closer until the noise is loud and clear in my ear. I detect a pungency in the air which quickly becomes fetid, and I almost choke on the next deep breath. Our sense of smell is hardwired to emotions, and that stench holds nothing but fear for me. Unsettled, I increase my pace sharply and put some distance between me and the danger. The beeping slows up, and a voice assures me I am clear – for now. The music kicks back in to keep up the motivation as my shredded nerves settle.

The zombies are not real, of course. However, the run, the anglers, the towpath, the smartphone and the earbuds are. To misquote contemporary Japanese writer Haruki Murakami, this is what I think about when I think about running. I'm using a running application called *Zombies, Run!* It's part audiobook, part fitness monitor, part zombie chase game. The narrative describes scenarios in a post-apocalyptic world where small communities survive marauding zombies by relying on a network of runners who keep survivor camps supplied with food and medicines. The zombie chase element relies on location and running pace to add threat of a gory ending at the hands of the undead to spur on a runner whose motivation might be temporarily lacking. It sounds implausible, far-fetched even. However, on a misty morning or at dusk, the zombie-like groaning of a voice actor is surprisingly real. It has, on more than one occasion, increased my heart rate, my average pace, and left me wishing that I had a cushion to hide behind.

There are many technologies at play to make this piece of digital ephemera work. It needs a mobile device with a powerful processor and packed full of technology, including GPS, just to make the application run. Four powerful technology waves – social, mobile, cloud and analytics, referred to by industry analysts Gartner as the *nexus of forces* – are driving transformational change in our personal and professional lives, including applications, or *apps*, like this. *Zombies, Run!*, whilst seemingly an inconsequential oddity, is a new type of app. It's groundbreaking in its own way. Its purpose is not functional, nor is it, strictly speaking, entertainment. It's neither game nor office tool. Instead, its purpose is to encourage – to do nothing more than motivate.

There are many people to thank for helping me keep up the motivation to write. Firstly, Jonathan Norman, who is as inspired by my twin passions of people and technology as I am. Then there are those who have worked with me on my own digital incentive project: David Estall, Michael Hodson, Adrian Hodsdon and Ricky Mistry, who developed the concept; Steve Borthwick, Richard Clark, Gary Hodsdon and Rachel Oldroyd, who built it into a product; Andrew Yates, who believed the idea into existence, which is what entrepreneurs do routinely – it's astonishing to witness – then Mike Blackadder, Kellie Lucas, Alastair Brown, Andy Sadler and Aanya Ali, who took ideas that would otherwise be too 'out there' to a sceptical market and made them coherent and compelling to our customers. We, and many other people at Artesian, took the crazy notion that we could measure the degree to which professional sales people are more focused on their customers than they are their own agenda and made it a digital reality. Not too shabby.

The community spirit is alive and well, and also played its part in getting this book to you. This includes those involved in the London Gamifiers, led by Toby Beresford and Andrzej Marczewski. It also includes those who blog, podcast, speak, write and generally share freely to allow us to engage in global conversations about this important topic. Amongst the many are Jesse Lahey, John Ferrara, Daniel Debow, Ian Bogost, Amy Jo Kim, Nicole Lazzaro, Gabe Zichermann, Jesse Schell, Kevin Werbach and Jon Radoff, and also two entrepreneurs from the UK CloudApps organisation: Simon Wheeldon and Peter Grant. They are doing remarkable things in the field of organisational motivation, and are making it a lot of fun, too.

Finally, it is the people closest to you who are required to give the most when you have a career and spend your spare time at a desk writing a book for your own (and hopefully, the readers') pleasure. I am blessed by their understanding, encouragement and inspiration.

PART I
Work and Play

Chapter 1

Game Changer

The Game

The neologism *gamification* was introduced in 2002 by British consultant Nick Pelling to describe how his business at the time, Conundra, developed electronic devices that were more like entertainment platforms. Only much later did it come to describe software rather than hardware, supplanting other terms such as *funware* that didn't gather the same momentum. Somewhat ironically, Pelling intended it to be an ugly word. For this he should be awarded maximum points, given the 'Mission Accomplished' badge and placed at the top of the leaderboard for awkward neologisms. It's a genuine ugly duckling, growing up to be a swan in 2011, when it was runner-up for the *Oxford English Dictionary* word of the year, after which it stuck. However, its acceptance is by no means certain. Many pioneers in this field still use the term reluctantly, and others, particularly the growing number of gamification software vendors, actively avoid using it with their customers for fear that the flippant phrase will diminish what they do. The term invites hype from some and frequent predictions that it is 'game over for gamification' from others.

However, gamification is much more than a word only its mother could love. Behind the inelegant phraseology is a set of underlying principles that are certain to gain momentum and widespread usage as the discipline matures and becomes better understood.

Gamification or whatever word that may or may not ultimately replace it is the use of elements we usually associate with fun and games to motivate, engage and change our behaviours in situations that are not games. But where did the idea originate? What's behind its becoming rapidly and widely discussed, and what's its potential to change our lives at home and at work?

The Badges

- Causal Cadet

- Digital Interventionista

- Fitness Coach

- Human Seller

- Moonshooter

To Know the Cause of Things

On a frosty February evening, I stood outside the New Academic Building of the London School of Economics (LSE), admiring the stone-crafted motto 'rerum cognoscere causas', or 'to know the causes of things'. It's also the name of a course that's compulsory for all LSE undergraduates, to introduce them to the fundamentals of thinking like a social scientist, examining the 'big' questions like 'How do we manage climate change?', Is population growth a threat or an opportunity?' and 'Who caused the financial crisis? It was fitting to be hosted by an institution that has, at its core, a grounding in examining important issues through different lenses.

I was waiting for the rest of a group of gamifiers, a London-based network of designers, consultants, writers and entrepreneurs involved in the world of gamification. At this stage, some readers may still be bristling at the words 'gamifiers' and 'gamification' even after understanding their origins. These synthetic terms may still be provoking a reaction that the nature of gamification is itself an altogether unnatural construction. Professor Kevin Werbach, Associate Professor at the Wharton School and co-author with Dan Hunter of *For the Win*, describes gamification as 'the use of game elements in a non-game context'. And it's this, rather than the word itself, that for many is jarring. Games, and particularly video games, are strictly leisure. They're a distraction or an escape. They have no place in the 'real world'. It makes no sense to weld game elements onto things that are not games. Like the world-renowned Ubon restaurants introduced by Nobuyuki Matsuhisa and Robert De Niro, who fused Japanese with Peruvian food, it shouldn't work. Except it does. And there's growing evidence to suggest that, when implemented correctly, it works well.

Eventually, when our group of gamifiers was quorate, we were ushered into a wood-panelled room by a team of masters students. The team were working on a project for an undisclosed bank to investigate the use of gamification to encourage children to develop a responsible attitude to money and savings.

The group had been invited to help shape the direction of the project. Whilst the bank was clearly an early innovator in this space, this wasn't the first group to think about the financial literacy of young people. The mobile game *Green$treets: Unleash the Loot!* was created by US author Neale Godfrey to do the same thing. Under-tens can earn money by completing chores, and can spend money in a marketplace on their mission to rescue and care for animals. They can also choose to save money in the *Green$treets* bank to pay for more expensive items later. The game sends progress notification emails to parents or carers so that adults can reinforce learning as it happens, and therefore at the point when their children will be most interested. Our group had been asked to inform the project with insights into what drives engagement in gaming and what it is that makes some games so compelling that their appeal is glibly described as 'addictive'. In addition, we identified which games attract children and the efficacy of educational games. Inputs came thick and fast from the group and from multiple perspectives. The various lenses of design, engineering, financial and commercial provided lively debate. A subsequent session drilled deeper into motivations. The group discussed and ranked the relative importance of game mechanics, which included reward, content, progression, community and customisation for two age ranges: one aged 7–12, and the other 13–16. The group also shared their experiences of existing games and how engaging they are, to identify whether the product should be influenced by elements found in, say, *Monopoly* or *FarmVille*.

In addition to the input from the community of gamifiers, the LSE team devised an online poll to harvest the opinions and ideas of others, including parents, on what they thought might be the best way to motivate children to learn about positive money management. As was fitting for the subject matter, this group of LSE masters students had complemented traditional approaches with contemporary digital ones, including connecting, crowdsourcing and co-creating with online communities.

Digital Interventions

Only a few weeks after the sessions with LSE, I joined a group in a very different setting. At the centre of London's 'Silicon Roundabout' is a Google facility which has all of Shoreditch's rich history on the outside, but is all industrial chic on the inside. This group meeting here, the largest such group in the UK, were a truly multidisciplinary lot. Sociologists, clinicians, healthcare consultants and biologists mixed with designers, technologists and entrepreneurs, all dedicated to debating how to bring about positive societal change using similarly technological and networked techniques. This group, District Health, are interested in the usage of technology as an enable for behavioural change in healthcare. They don't use the word 'gamification', at least not any more. The group, formerly known as Gamify Your Health, prefer the term 'digital intervention'. Their vision is to improve health by helping the nation live the adage 'prevention is better than cure'. Their experience is that healthcare costs less the further away from hospital it's delivered. It's also best for us as individuals. In his book *Zen Habits*, former journalist and blogger Leo Babauta makes a commonsense point about living healthily. If you don't live and eat well, if you regularly indulge in fatty, greasy, salty or sugary foods, then you'll almost certainly have higher healthcare needs over time. That means frequent visits to the pharmacist, the doctor's surgery, the hospital, even the operating theatre. Being unhealthy is, amongst other things, a complication that we would all be better off without. The District Health group want to find innovative new ways to help individuals create healthier habits, and to have fun in the process.

Today's theme is a somewhat sensitive one. At first blush – and there's an intended pun here – it would seem unlikely that we can intervene with technology to influence what is one of the most basic of human drives. We're debating how to promote the use of condoms among those young men who fall into the socio-economic group most likely to engage in risky sexual activity.

An insight into a previous project, the website Sexunzipped and some unsettling insights into the rising rates of sexually transmitted infections immediately raise the energy level in the room. Nervous, salacious, childish or prurient thoughts are displaced by the seriousness of the subject and the forthright and intelligent introduction to the session from Dr Julia Bailey from University College London. As is common with gamification projects, we first establish a *persona* – a profile, sometimes called a player type, that describes the target group for the intervention. Our persona is James. James is 19, Afro-Caribbean, lives in a poor inner-city area in London, and would describe himself as 'very heterosexual'. His mum, proud and hardworking in our extended persona description, would be extremely upset if James became a father too early. She believes in social mobility, and has aspirations for James that include further education, a profession and material success outside of her own experiences.

Persona established and debated, we quickly get on to the design workshops. Eight or nine groups of four people around the room focus on interventions that might normalise condom usage, deal with the perceived reduction in pleasure, and address the embarrassment associated with buying and using condoms. The air is alive with debate. In our group and the groups around us there are questions, like 'How do we help young women confidently veto sex without condoms?', 'How do we help young men not to feel undermined by discussions about condom size?' and 'How can we encourage young men and women to be prepared before the "moment" without them being labelled promiscuous?' Ideas are thrown around like confetti. One group settles on a mobile phone app that will allow young men to use their mobile phone camera to measure their penis, recommend their condom size, and offer statistics that assure them that their machismo isn't undermined whatever their dimensions. Another group debate a geolocator app that immediately identifies those in a bar or club who have identified themselves as prepared and sexually responsible by carrying protection and making this status visible. Other ideas are formed and shaped in the room until there's a wall full of Post-it Notes that will later be voted on. Any one of these ideas may later be developed into an interactive questionnaire, website, mobile app or other digital intervention to modify one of the strongest, most vital and compelling human drives.

Gamification Origins

Both these initiatives are about future projects – two of many examples of growing corporate, government and academic interest in how the use of digital interventions and gamification can influence customers, citizens and society to promote profit, civic-mindedness and the greater good. Such interest stems from the rise of high-profile online and mobile gamified systems. However, the principles aren't really new. Gamification has been with us since at least 1981, the year American Airlines launched a programme that's still very much alive and well today: AAdvantage.

Tom Stuker, a 59-year-old trainer, can testify to this. His prize for winning this particular game is an almost complete absence of queuing. On 6 December 2012, on a flight from London to Chicago on United Airlines, Stuker reached 1,000,000 miles in a single year. United's Premier Elite status requires travellers to fly 100,000 miles in a year. Stuker had achieved that and, as United's top flier, he also had a total of 13,000,000 miles under his belt, which he undoubtedly keeps buckled just in case of turbulence. Interestingly, in an interview with Joe Sharkey for the *New York Times*, Stuker was obviously keeping an eye on his rival, Fred Finn, a British expatriate in his early seventies who has flown 15,000,000 miles. He warns Finn to look over his shoulder, because he intends to overtake him within a couple of years. Like George Clooney's Ryan Bingham in Jason Reitman's film *Up in the Air*, it's not entirely clear whether Stuker collects the miles because he flies, or whether he flies because he collects the miles.

Figure 1.1   Frequent flyer
Source: Creative Commons, Larry Johnson, 'Ten toes over the line … Elite Status!', September 2010. https://creativecommons.org/licenses/by/2.0/.

Stuker isn't alone, of course. Around 120 million people are collecting frequent flyer miles. They're earning points. Those who are particularly good at collecting points in a set period, usually annually, will 'level up'. For Virgin Atlantic's Flying Club, this means moving from red to silver and then on to the top-tier world of gold. Stuker is an example of how much the colour of a card and a change in status represented by free on-board cocktails and special check-in arrangements can motivate us to choose one provider over another at what may be increased personal and financial cost.

Thirty years on, and frequent flyer programmes continue to leverage game elements such as points and levels in a way that has changed very little, yet they remain a potent marketing device. The use of status, associated with being an elite flyer or an American Express Black Card holder, has become increasingly sophisticated and has splintered into endless varieties. I'm a frequent user of the location-based social and mobile app *Foursquare*, and I was genuinely excited to have unlocked the 'Warhol' badge after checking into the Tate Modern's Lichtenstein Retrospective in February 2013. I was equally thrilled when I unlocked a 'Zoetrope' badge for checking in to ten movie theatres, a 'Jobs' badge for checking in at three different Apple retail stores, and a 'Banksy' badge which required not only that I attended the movie *Exit Through the Gift Shop*, but that I also mentioned Banksy in my status update. Foursquare later reinvented badges when it split its applications into *Foursquare* and *Swarm*, but these small, imaginatively crafted personal achievements make counting miles seem primitive by comparison.

Habit-changing

Frequent flyer schemes and *Foursquare* are examples of gamified marketing and the use of game mechanics to influence our habits as consumers. The same approach can be used to rail against a sedentary lifestyle.

A typical working day for me involves nothing more strenuous than mouse clicks and eye strain. Like many in similar jobs of a similar age, I run. These days, I find it relaxing, meditative and enjoyable. I return from a weekend run brimming with energy and positively glowing. However, it wasn't always this way. It required me to build new habits, fresh patterns of positive behaviour. Like all new behaviours, it was at first uncomfortable and hard to keep up. What helped was something that increased my engagement in this new activity that was also a lot of fun. In the Preface, I described an app, *Zombies, Run!*, which was as familiar to the District Health group as it was to me – part audiobook, part fitness monitor, part zombie chase game. The imaginary threat of an untimely end as an entree for al fresco zombie diners helped me past the difficult stage after the first couple of weeks, where persistence is required to make it a permanent lifestyle change.

Not everyone requires extreme motivations such as an untimely and horrible death to achieve their personal best. Almost two million runners use Nike+ to monitor their distance, pace and calories burned. Digital rewards such as encouragement from celebrity contributors act as rewards for reaching milestones. After a workout with Nike+, runners go online, where their data has been automatically uploaded and they can track their statistics, set new goals, sign up for challenges and connect with the community of runners. Other similar applications, such as *RunKeeper*, *Strava*, *Fitocracy* and *Run Or Else*, which makes charity donations as a penalty for missed commitments, are an indication of how gamified applications have become part of our fitness regimes.

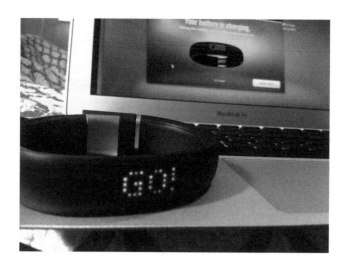

Figure 1.2   Nike+ FuelBand
Source: Creative Commons, The Pug Father, 'Nike+ Fuelband unboxing'. https://creativecommons.org/licenses/by/2.0/.

An important feature of these apps is that they allow the player to be in control. The route to success is not step-by-step, prescriptive or rigid. A personal best is just that – personal. One runner might be looking to improve their pace, another distance, another to reach a target weight. Well-designed gamified applications mandate only the broadest of objectives, allow players to shape what their details and how they intend to reach them. This is one of our first clues about the appeal of gamification and how it can motivate us as individuals in a way that a gameless activity may not.

Playing Outside

Gamification is challenging the notion that games are the reason behind a generation of couch potatoes. Take *Zamzee* – which, like our kids' and finance project, aims to establish early positive behaviours.

Figure 1.3   *Zamzee*
Source: Creative Commons, Zach Copley, 'Fancy green lights come on when I plug it into USB'. https://creativecommons.org/licenses/by-sa/2.0/.

For a one-off payment, parents are given an activity meter which fits into their children's pockets or can be attached to their clothes. The meter automatically updates a *Zamzee* account with daily activities. Points (inevitably called pointz) are awarded for extra activities like attending gym class or taking the family dog for a walk. Pointz lead to badges and positions on a leaderboard. Among the most popular features of *Zamzee* are the challenges. These are themed, story-based adventures such as 'Escape from Alcatraz' that award bonus points for taking part.

Good Gaming, or Gaming for Good

Zamzee is also doing something of a public relations job for the gaming world. It's reversing the perception, particularly of parents, that video games are an entirely a bad thing, to be reduced, removed or rationed like all other unhealthy treats. Others have tried before, most notably with a genre of educational games that were neither fun nor particularly enlightening. With notable exceptions, this field of gaming pleased neither parent nor child, and is itself going through a renaissance as a result of new gamification thinking.

The ambitions of some gamification projects, though, are grander. They look beyond the self, and aspire to make the world a better place. One such platform, Greenbean Recycle, is a startup that's working on recycling on the campuses of some of the USA's most prestigious universities, such as MIT and Harvard. The solution includes elements of analytics, social media and game mechanics to divert materials from landfill using intercollegiate rivalry as the primary motivation. Their website keeps a real-time log of kilowatt hours saved by, say, Harvard compared to MIT or the University of South Indiana to keep the competition real and alive.

When Chris Osborne, Product Manager at AlertMe, spoke at the *Big Data Week* conference in London in April 2013, he observed that most of us have a very distant understanding of home energy consumption. There's little connection between the statement we receive once every three months and how we use it in our homes. We simply don't think about energy in that way. Much of our energy consumption is invisible: the pilot light on the boiler, our refrigerator and water heating. Consciously, we charge our mobile devices, use the tumble dryer when it's wet outside and sit in front of a laptop or television into the early hours. The disconnect between our activity at home and a quarterly report makes it very difficult to influence behaviours around energy usage.

The Facebook of green gamification, Opower, is trying to fix this. Opower is an independent software business partnered with utility providers that keeps a running score of the kilowatt hours saved and carbon dioxide abated on its home page. The numbers are significant. Most impactful is the quarter of a billion dollars that they have saved off utility bills for their subscribers. Opower, somewhat counter-intuitively, mails paper reports that detail the household's energy consumption, the times of day when most energy is being consumed and which appliances are being most wasteful. The report also includes a chart which compares your own energy use to your community average. Finally, you're rated with two smiley faces for consuming less than 80 per cent of the community average, one smiley face for using less than average, and none for using more than average. There's no frowny face – at least, not any more.

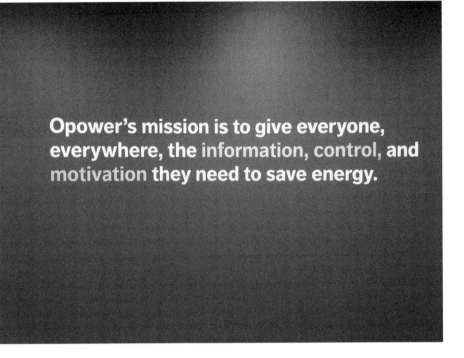

Figure 1.4   Opower

Source: Creative Commons, Ted Eytan, 'OPOWER 17590'. https://creativecommons.org/licenses/by/2.0/.

This form of gamification gives us another clue as to its potency. The numbers, comparisons and emoticons are all designed to provide effective feedback. What's more, the feedback has a direct and obvious link to activity. In turn, positive changes to activity result in highly correlated and motivating feedback.

Gamification of Work

Gary Hamel has been ranked by the *Wall Street Journal* as the world's most influential business thinker. He was responsible for bringing 36 other management experts together at Half Moon Bay, California to create a series of aspirational objectives that would inspire innovation in the world of business. The event was organised by Management Lab, supported by McKinsey, and brought together an impressive list of thought leaders, academics, analysts, consultants and CEOs, from whom emerged 25 'moonshots'. Each is on a critical path in the journey to reinventing management, each one intending to inspire green-shoots thinking, fresh ways of working and create new management innovators. The ninth moonshot is *Taking the Work out of Work*. It reads:

> *Human Beings are most productive when work feels like play. Enthusiasm, imagination and resourcefulness get unleashed when people are having fun. In the future the most successful organisations will be the ones that have learned to blur the line between work and play. In practice, this may mean allowing individuals to choose their own work, turning repetitive tasks into the equivalent of online, multiplayer games, or creating roles that encompass a great variety of tasks. Over the past century, enormous progress has been made in engineering the inefficiencies out of work; now management innovators must engineer the drudgery out of work. (Gary Hamel,* What Matters Now, *pp. 248–9)*

That's right. Representatives from Google, Harvard, MIT and London Business School, along with leading authorities in the world of business such as Henry Mintzberg, Andrew McAfee, Eric Schmidt, Marissa Mayer and Terry Kelly, arrived at the conclusion that future successful businesses would be making work more like online multiplayer games.

Nike built the Nike+ platform to engage fitness enthusiasts. Zamzee use gamification to help families increase their physical activity. Opower use gamification to change household energy consumption patterns. The list of applications for gamification is continuing to grow, and is also making its mark on the corporate world. In their *Top Predictions for IT Organisations and Users for 2013 and Beyond,* Industry analysts Gartner suggested that four out of ten of the Global 1,000 organisations will be using gamification as the primary device to transform operational processes in 2015, and that it won't stop there.

New Skills

When habits form, according to Charles Duhigg in his book *The Power of Habit,* our brains no longer fully participate in the decision-making process. They become automatic. This is one of the reasons why it's difficult to stop bad habits and start new and positive ones. However, once we create a new pattern of using novel skills, regular exercise, healthy eating or positive behaviours, they become unconscious, powerful and sometimes life-changing.

Using the powerful photograph image manipulation software *Photoshop* is daunting for those on the first day of their free thirty-day trial. Many will stare at the array of buttons, menus and options and their mind will go as blank as the white canvas all of these options engulfs them. Petar Karafezov, Digital Marketing Manager at Adobe, was well aware that the software company needed to get their trial users, or trialists, through that early pain barrier, after which they inevitably became proficient and loyal users. He turned to games for inspiration. The result was *LevelUp*, a game of missions that leads trialists through basic techniques to improve their photos. Before the trialists know it, they have remedied red eyes, whitened teeth, removed unwanted objects and created the perfect portrait. The approach, sometimes referred to as 'cascading information', releases information at the point when it's needed, and not before.

New Behaviours

The same *motivational hump* that needs to be conquered to develop new skills must also be addressed when change is introduced to communities of employees, customers, or both. Artesian Solutions is an innovator in social customer relationship management. Its platform provides highly relevant insights to sales professionals about their prospective customers. If an international business reports disappointing results and one of the reasons is the strong pound, a business banking specialist, usually referred to as a relationship manager, can choose to be alerted. This is an opportunity for the relationship manager to help with foreign exchange advice and discuss products or services that will no doubt be welcomed by a management team under pressure from their investors. This is indicative of an approach referred to as 'social selling', which is about connecting with customers when they most need help, rather than the archaic and hugely unpopular practice of interrupting business people with unsolicited emails or cold calls. The use of Artesian insights requires that professional sellers replace old behaviours with new ones, and that they're entirely driven by customer needs rather than traditional selling techniques, product launches and old-style direct marketing. It requires a leap of faith that all those small changes each day will ultimately result in success.

The team at Artesian are continually working on new ideas to motivate its users through the period of change, and one such idea was a traditional business tool: the management dashboard. The dashboard would help sales managers understand who was and wasn't using the service. The challenge with this was that it would result in traditional carrot-and-stick incentivisation for an approach grounded in individual autonomy. We wanted individuals to be personally motivated, so we developed a scoring system that measured how customer-focused the individual was being. We examined the thousands of ways in which they interacted with the Artesian service, and identified patterns that indicated that users were being targeted in approaching their prospective customers, rather than interrupting them with cold calls. We then measured the degree to which they became conversant with their customers' businesses rather than their own. Finally, we measured the frequency with which they engaged in open and collaborative sharing. The scoring system used signals derived from activity to measure customer-centricity. A higher score indicated that sellers were trying to do all the right things by understanding and engaging with their customers on their customers' terms. The integrity of the score was important, so the algorithms ensured that interactions were authentic and that behaviours were changing naturally over time, rather than in temporary or short-term bursts. Gamification elements included leaderboards intended to help peer groups compare notes, rather than management controls. Every time the system was rolled out, we saw a strong correlation between high scorers and those highly regarded by their customers. It didn't matter whether it was financial services or media sales, the results were the same. The newly implemented score encouraged greater use of the service to get closer to and better understand customers.

Figure 1.5   Artesian social seller score

Mission Roundup

There are a growing number of applications that encourage us to lace up our running shoes, eat one less blueberry muffin, turn off a light or generally lead a healthier life. The number of gamified applications or digital interventions that can influence our behaviours is increasing, and increasing rapidly as the technology that makes it possible becomes commonplace.

Businesses, too, are discovering new applications using the gamified approach. These fall into a class of applications that are *systems of engagement*. Traditional systems, *systems of record*, allow businesses to get things done.

They efficiently generate orders, ship products and raise invoices. Systems of engagement, rather than creating transactional efficiencies, create improvements in the quality of interactions. They improve customer and employee engagement in the shape of loyalty and productivity.

Zamzee and Nike+ change how we think about our lifestyle, Opower and Greenbean the way we think about recycling and energy. Enterprise applications such as *LevelUp* and the Artesian *Social Seller Score* help us adapt to new skills and habits when we might otherwise revert to old and outdated patterns. The growing use of such systems is a recognition that people are multi-dimensional rather than predictable consumers, sales targets or worker bees. Organisations and the processes that run them are evolving to reflect this in the form of more human and social systems.

Finally, gamification is a means of achieving personal success. It's about the attainment of individual goals. This assumes that employee, customer, investor and community goals are all aligned, of course. However, the most influential businesses are successful for that very reason.

Chapter 2
Carrots, Sticks, Nudges and Fun

The Game

The VP of Sales wasn't getting the information she needed from the newly implemented customer relationship management application. She couldn't find contact information for new accounts, and it was unclear when she met with customers whether the last contact from her team had been last week, last month or last year. She could always ask, of course, and she did, but the team spent most of their time travelling or working from their home office, so it always took longer to find out basic information than it should. What was worse was that she was never confident about her forecasts. This required every single member of the team to enter their opportunities accurately, and few did. Somewhat frustrated, she implemented controls and processes which most, but not all, followed. Finally, in order to achieve the full adoption that was needed, she applied a single simple rule: If opportunities aren't captured accurately, then they don't exist. Commissions can only be paid on deals that exist, likewise only real deals can count towards quota attainment, and this means ensuring they're all 'on the system'.

She found everyone compliant, but grudgingly so. Whilst she now had the information she needed, she had created a whole host of new problems. The team didn't really understand the value of the information they were being asked to capture. Instead of finding time to creatively blend the new system into their working day, the team let other things slide. No one was expecting the team to do everything, but the VP couldn't help feeling that more things were being sacrificed than really needed to be. On reflection, she decided that the number of difficult conversations and morale issues were problems that might otherwise have been avoided.

I've heard this story and variations of it many times from companies of all sizes from dozens of industries. Managers need their teams to co-operate in ways that aren't immediately apparent, so inducements or corrections inevitably follow when instruction fails. Are there really only two tools available to align individuals to the goals of the organisation? In the twenty-first century, are we still relying on little more than incentive and punishment? Is the modern organisation, and the people that comprise it, relying on tools as primitive as the carrot and the stick?

The Badges

- *Homo Economicus*

- Choice Architect

- Calculating Criminal

- Stair Taker

Economic Man

In *Decision Sourcing*, Rooven Pakkiri and I assert that businesses are, like all social structures, organised around a common purpose – economic activity. In fact, economic activity could even have been a critical part in human evolutionary development. Neanderthals, hairy strong and tough, as was appropriate for Ice Age conditions, had a 200,000-year run before *Homo sapiens* arrived. Ten thousand years later, they were gone. The prevailing theory is that modern man had sophisticated tools, making him better at hunting and warring. Research by Jason Shogren of the University of Wyoming and Gardner M. Brown of the University of Washington suggests that, rather than toolmaking, it was trade that was behind *Homo sapiens* dominating previous members of the genus. Brown and Shogren's research, reported in the *Journal of Economic Perspectives*, suggests that the early survival of humanity depended upon economic co-operation. *Homo sapiens*'s edge came from collaboration, trading and specialisation of labour. Whilst Neanderthal Man hunted hard, *Homo sapiens*'s system allowed bad hunters to hang up their spears and become craftsmen or take on other useful roles. Specialisation and a system of exchange increased their share of the finite amount of meat and other resources. The rest, according to Brown and Shogren, is evolutionary history.

Consumers and Producers

Economic activity might have perpetuated our species, but it also, partly at least, defines us. Since Adam Smith's landmark work popularly known as *The Wealth of Nations*, economics has been used to explain human behaviour through two primary activities: consumption and production. Human behaviour and the design of the modern business are inseparable. Marketing and sales disciplines are built around understanding us as consumers, whilst workforce and performance management want to define us as producers.

Businesses today are built on assumptions derived from a largely unchanged neoclassical view of economics, in which we behave logically, rationally and usually in our own interests. Nineteenth-century, British philosopher and economist John Stuart Mill is credited with introducing this view of human motivation through economics. In his essay 'On the Definition of Political Economy; and on the Method of Investigation Proper To It', he suggests that:

> Political Economy presuppose[s] an arbitrary definition of man, as a being who invariably does that by which he may obtain the greatest amount of necessaries, conveniences, and luxuries, with the smallest quantity of labour and physical self-denial with which they can be obtained. (para. 46)

Mill is sometimes mistakenly credited with introducing the term 'Economic Man', or *Homo economicus*, when in fact it was his critics who used it as shorthand for Mill's definition of a human as one who attempts to maximise utility as a consumer and economic profit as a producer. Economic Man wants as many carrots as possible for least effort.

This view has had its critics, of course. Peter Drucker wrote *The End of the Economic Man* in 1939, which was neither the first nor the last challenge. This rational and logical view is a robust theory, and does go some way to explain human behaviour. However, it is, in practice, anomalous. Take, for example, a classic economic experiment, *The Ultimatum Game*, which involves two players determining how to divide up a sum of money. The first player proposes how to divide the money between the two players, and the second can either accept or reject the proposal. If the second player rejects the proposal, neither player receives any money at all, and the game can only be played once, to remove reciprocity as an influence. In study after study, offers of less than 20 per cent from the first player are routinely rejected by the second. The second player is choosing to reject something – in fact, the maximum they could possibly receive at this point. It really shouldn't matter to *Homo economicus* if he's receiving only $5 out of a pool of $150, since it's the only game in town. However, in practice it clearly does. *The Ultimatum Game* hints that our motivations don't solely concern economic gain.

Rational Criminology

The fact that we don't act rationally, economically speaking, was the subject of a 1983 paper 'Choices, Values and Frames' by Daniel Kahneman, an Israeli-American psychologist and Nobel laureate, along with Amos Tversky, an expert in human judgement. What they discovered was that people's attitudes regarding risks associated with gains are different to those associated with losses. The economically rational choice between definitely getting $1,000 or a 50 per cent chance of getting $2,500 is to accept the risk. It's calculably the better deal. However, Kahneman and Tversky discovered that more people accept the $1,000. In doing so, they introduced the theory of *loss aversion* and founded the field of behavioural economics.

Dan Ariely, the author who popularised behavioural economics in *Predictably Irrational* and *The Upside of Irrationality*, offered an extreme example of rational economic models of human behaviour in a later book. In *The (Honest) Truth about Dishonesty*, Ariely introduces his readers to the Simple Model Of Rational Crime (SMORC) from University of Chicago economist Gary Becker. Becker, a Nobel laureate, suggests that people commit crime based on a rational, economic evaluation of each situation. If the probability of getting caught for illegal parking multiplied by the cost of the parking ticket is less than the cost of parking legally, then people will take the risk. Take the model through its paces and it suggests that if we needed the money, our decision about whether or not to stage a bank robbery would be based on the likelihood of its successful execution and the costs associated with getting caught, factored by the probability of this happening. This may be an exercise in *reductio ad absurdum*, but it illustrates that the reason why the overwhelming majority of us don't rob banks has little to do with economics or the cost–benefit case.

In truth, even Mill knew it to be an abstraction that failed to capture the whole human motive. Measured by a strict economic framework, our choices, rather than being rational, can seem partly, and sometimes wholly, irrational. According to the New Economics Foundation, an independent 'think and do tank', other factors include social influence, habits, values, imperfect computation and a desire to be involved and do the right thing. There's more to us than a ledger of inputs and outputs.

Carrots and Sticks

The notion that our behaviour as consumers can't be completely explained by rational economics has gained momentum and acceptance. It's the subject of any number of popular publications, including William Poundstone's *Priceless: The Hidden Psychology of Value*, Barry Schwartz's *The Paradox of Choice* and Paco Underhill's *Why We Buy: The Science of Shopping*. However, what's also open to scrutiny is our behaviour as producers. The same individuals who are customers are also the employees that turn up at the workplace each and every morning.

Businesses, in their efforts to maximise production, use the tools of classic economics too. Employers reward behaviour they want more of, and punish behaviour they want to reduce. They use financial incentives, bonuses and commissions as carrots whilst holding disciplinary processes, perhaps even termination of employment, as sticks. Malcolm Tucker, the fictional and monstrously profane politician and Director of Communications in the film *In the Loop* and the BBC television satirical series *The Thick of It* famously had his own carrot-and-stick approach: 'You take the carrot and you stick it [somewhere painful], followed by the stick, followed by an even bigger and rougher carrot.' Whilst everyone recognises Tucker as a comedic figure, there's a skewed view of people in positions of power that hasn't really been helped by reality shows such as *The Apprentice*. On both sides of the Atlantic, Donald Trump and Alan Sugar, as what we can only hope are pantomime versions of themselves, veer between six-figure job offers and growling 'You're fired' at contestants. Whilst extremes exist largely in satire and caricature, the fundamental methods of employee motivation remain distinctly orange-coloured or stick-like. Leaders set the business direction, then executives work with Human Resources to align management team compensation. In turn, middle managers design individual compensation plans and payment by objectives for their teams. On the often tenuous assumption that the compensation of individual contributors, managers, directors and executives all align without creating overlap or competition, then the business grows and everyone is rewarded for their part through achieving goals and realising bonuses and cash payments.

As we look around a typical business for boxes of carrots, we're most likely to see the largest stack outside the Sales Department. Professional sellers are easy to measure. The more revenue they generate, the more they are rewarded. It's not uncommon for sales representatives to take on a package where commission makes up half or more of their potential earnings. It's not all carrot, either. One former professional seller shared with me what it was like to sell photocopiers when he started out. He had weekly targets, and bad weeks weren't tolerated. Those who didn't 'make their number' were forced to hand in the keys to their company cars. They could think about strategies for improving their performance on the bus ride home before explaining to their families that their weekend plans would be somewhat reined in because of their temporarily reduced mobility. This is probably unsurprising to most of us, and it impacts how we perceive sellers. For his book *To Sell is Human*, Daniel Pink commissioned a survey of almost 10,000 respondents to find out what they did at work, including the elements of their role that were sales-related. In doing so, he also posed the question 'What is the first word that comes to mind when you think of sales?' He then removed the nouns, which were largely value-neutral synonyms for selling, and was left with a word cloud of adjectives. The rule with word (or tag) clouds is that the more frequently a word is mentioned, the larger and heavier the font. The most prominent word was 'pushy'. Many, including 'sleazy', 'difficult' and 'dishonest', barely concealed popular distaste. Of the 25 words offered, only five had a positive connotation. Decades of neoclassical motivation have reduced the common view of usually intelligent, honest, hard-working and ethical individuals to one of double-dealing duplicity.

Nudges

Our unfailingly rational Economic Man, assuming the incentives or penalties are right, can be guided to work hard, stay within the speed limit, reduce his carbon footprint, eat healthily, exercise regularly and place his empty bottles into a bin destined for recycling rather than landfill. Humans, meanwhile, with their flawed rationality, are less predictable. They can't be manipulated reliably with cash payments or spot fines. In fact, a branch of behavioural economics argues that we can be more effectively influenced without direct instruction. We don't need to rely on the most common forms of stick – legislation and enforcement – we can be *nudged*.

The most famous example in *Nudge*, Richard Thaler and Cass Sunstein's definitive book on the subject, can be found in the men's bathrooms at Amsterdam's Schiphol Airport. A realistic sketch of a housefly has been etched on each urinal, right next to the drain. Apparently, men are easily distracted when urinating, which in a busy airport bathroom is a significant and unpleasant problem. However, men are also, for some reason, naturally inclined to aim, and the housefly motif resulted in a decline in spillage of 80 per cent. That one tiny nudge has achieved what countless signs in offices all around the world imploring co-workers to leave the bathroom in a decent state for the next person have not.

Nudges have been designed to help people save for retirement, make healthier eating choices and increase organ donations. In the UK, vehicle-activated signs which use the simplest of nudges – feedback – are being put to effective use in reducing speed. Accidents, being what they are – the random coincidence of multiple factors – are statistically difficult to measure. However, some reports suggest that digital signs that display simple messages to 'slow down' when exceeding the speed limit reduce accidents as effectively as their legislative cousins, speed enforcement cameras.

Fun Theory

In 2009, Swedish design company DDB along with car manufacturer Volkswagen launched *Rolighetsteorin*, or 'Fun Theory', an initiative to change behaviours not with carrots, sticks or nudges, but with fun. One of the most charming examples was implemented in the Odenplan subway station, located in the Vasastaden district in central Stockholm. I used this station myself on many occasions during a two-year secondment to the Swedish office of analytics business Cognos, now part of IBM. Stairs located right next to an escalator were replaced with working piano keys. The result was that 66 per cent more people used the piano keys than had used the stairs. Other successes included the 'world's deepest bin', which played a cartoon-like sound of plummeting each time a piece of rubbish was placed inside it.

The winning innovation, *Hastighetslotteriet*, or 'Speed Camera Lottery', was submitted by San Francisco game producer Kevin Richardson. The concept was put into action in collaboration with NTF, the Swedish road transport authority. A speed camera recorded driver speeds, and displayed either a thumbs up or a thumbs down in response. Those who exceeded the speed limit received a fine, which was paid into a lottery pool. Those who drove under the speed limit were entered into a draw to win the pool. Volkswagen claimed a victory for the initiative. Over three days, almost 25,000 cars passed the camera. The average speed was reduced from 32 km/hour before the experiment to 25 km/hour during it.

Mission Roundup

In 2003 a single directory enquiry service was replaced with hundreds of 118 numbers. The UK Government had put conventional economics into action to introduce competition, offer customers more choice and drive prices down.

The result was a hike in prices and a spike in complaints. Aditya Chakrabortty, consumer affairs economics commentator for *The Guardian*, reported in his article 'Why We Buy What We Buy' that even regulators later admitted that it was a shambles. Behavioural economists would have advised Whitehall differently. An understanding of the human condition recognises that if we are presented with too much choice or complexity we make poor decisions or do nothing.

Smart businesses are making use of insights from behaviouralists in designing the customer experience. In the *McKinsey Quarterly* article 'A Marketers Guide to Behavioural Economics' Ned Welch outlines a number of techniques that retailers routinely use. An Italian telecoms company, for example, dramatically reduced contract cancellations once they understood loss aversion. Instead of offering 100 free calls if they kept their plan, they credited the account with 100 calls up front and asked how the customer would use them. Many customers did not want to give up their free talk time when they felt they already owned it. Retailers are aware that allowing consumers to delay payment will dramatically increase their willingness to buy. Payments, like losses, are viscerally and somewhat irrationally unpleasant. So store cards, payment apps or even short payment delays soften the immediate sting of parting with money and remove the barrier to purchase.

These customers, though, are the very same people who make up the corporate workforce, yet the principles of incentive systems haven't really changed over the last two decades at all. They rely almost entirely on paying for motivation. Businesses implement ever more complex systems to align payment and incentives across the organisation but they fundamentally rely on a single unchanging principle. More production results in greater rewards. It's logical of course but individual quirks, psychology and human behaviour are ignored in favour of neoclassical economic theories. If, as Dan Ariely suggests, we are irrational consumers, then we are irrational employees too.

Chapter 3
Working for Free

The Game

Our days are spent engaging in a variety of pursuits. Some are routine and mundane, whilst others have the capacity to make hours seem like minutes, and have us pleading, like English singer-songwriter Fiona Bevan, 'please, time, go slo-mo'.

Some activity is its own reward, whilst we need a caffeine jolt, words of encouragement or monetary incentive to do others. Work is the most common activity requiring financial reward. Money is required to buy food, a home, clothing, healthcare and comforts, so we work. We exchange our labour, skills and time for a salary. On the surface, we work out of simple economics, but this doesn't explain why some are drawn to lower-paid vocational careers or why there's a wide variety in performance from individuals on comparable pay scales.

Does work need to be paid, and is it work if it isn't? Likewise, can it only be leisure that's fun, and does fun have to be easy? Can fun be work, and can work be fun?

The Badges

- Giffgaff Grafter

- Perfect Practiser

- Cognitive Contributor

- Philosopher of Fun

Paid Labour

We avoid becoming dull and unexciting, according to the proverb, by ensuring that fun displaces at least some of our daily toil. Labour is wearisome, whilst play is engaging. In addition, it would seem, taking part in it also makes us more interesting to others. That chocolate bar promises to help us with this balancing act by providing sufficient energy for work, rest and play, too. This implies that these three broad classes of daily activity are very separate. If they were illustrated in a Venn diagram, there would be no intersections: three separate and equal-sized circles. Play is fun, work is serious, and rest is the absence of the others. Play is easy, something we do voluntarily. Work is hard, and something for which we demand remuneration.

If we were asked to join the office five-a-side football team, we wouldn't ask about the hourly rate. Nor would we expect 'double time' to join a social club go-karting outing on a Sunday morning. We wouldn't, however, book a vacation day for a weekday afternoon spent networking with customers or business partners. We have a clear sense of work and play, and that the former is paid whilst the latter isn't. It's deeply ingrained in our values even though there are too many exceptions to prove it the rule.

In Mark Twain's novel *Tom Sawyer*, Tom is unhappy as he looks up, down and across Aunt Polly's thirty-yard-long and nine-feet-high fence. The reason is that, as punishment for spending the day by the river instead of in school, his aunt has set him the task of whitewashing it. This is the worst kind of labour. Not only is it looking long and arduous, but there will be no pay. Aunt Polly believes that Tom has already received his 'payment' in the form of an idle day, and according to Twain, Tom feels a sense of 'deep melancholia'. Of course, Sawyer is an inventive young man, so he attempts to shorten the work with the help of others. He first attempts to offer his friend Jim a 'white alley' marble to help, but he is caught in the act of negotiating the deal by his aunt, who chases off his potential helper. At this point Tom refines his plan, so that when another friend arrives, Ben Rogers, Tom tries an entirely different approach. Instead of offering to pay for Ben's help, Tom convinces Ben that whitewashing a fence is an 'adventure'. Implausibly, Tom is so convincing in his description of the activity that Ben even agrees to pay Tom an apple for the privilege. Emboldened by the success of the new strategy, Tom offers every other boy who passes by the same deal. It isn't long before the fence has three coats of whitewash and Tom has a collection of rewards as payment. What Tom discovered was that labour involved payment, albeit in marbles, in exchange for effort. Remove payment, and it was no longer labour. As Twain puts it:

'Work consists of whatever a body is obliged to do. Play consists of whatever a body is not obliged to do.'

This held true for industrial society, but is increasingly inaccurate in the post-industrial, knowledge-based and networked society. It doesn't adequately explain the behaviours of what Brian Solis, author of *The End of Business as Usual* calls 'the Connected Generation'. Solis is one of the first commentators on networked society to define a generation not by their age, but by their digital behaviours. Almost 2,000 of the Connected Generation have taken part in defining the subject of 'concrete' on Wikipedia. Many thousands of edits and hours have been spent on this subject alone. Is this activity, part of the estimated 100,000,000 hours spent creating Wikipedia, work, or is it play? Writing on the subject of a composite, coarse building material doesn't feel like play, but on the other hand, it doesn't qualify as work either. It's not, strictly speaking, a professional or occupational activity if it's unpaid.

Working for Free

Call centres are often the main point of interaction between companies and their customers after a purchase has been made. They have become synonymous with frustration. More than one in five of us describe our experiences of them as poor, according to a 2012 YouGov survey. They would seem, to most of us, to be a failed experiment in workplace social engineering. They seem irretrievably broken. However, one company has reversed the trend. Their customers love the level of service they receive from a company that employs no one to deliver it. Mobile phone network giffgaff has achieved a net promoter score in the same range, 73 per cent, as that of the gold standard of Apple and Google in customer satisfaction. Almost all support is provided by its community of customers, who enjoy a lower-cost service in return. They can also be rewarded with cash incentives and free calls. Whilst there are a handful of 'educators', giffgaff staff that guide the community, support is delivered each and every day without paying salaries.

Contributors to Wikipedia and the giffgaff community are producers who challenge all definitions of Economic Man. Instead, their productivity comes from within. They're intrinsically motivated. They're happy and willing to produce for almost nothing.

Hard Play

Whilst classifying contributions to Wikipedia and giffgaff support is problematic, there's no doubt about the nature of games. Games, particularly video games, are strictly play – a leisure pursuit in the same category as reading a Dan Brown novel or solitarily trying to rearrange a deck of cards through seven piles then finally into one pile for each suit. *World of Warcraft* (*WoW*), for example, is manifestly not work. In fact, it's precisely its dissimilarity to work that makes it so popular. Surely? Not according to Swedish ethnologist Peder Stenberger. Stenberger played a full 250 days of *WoW* whilst researching his thesis on the social impact of playing *WoW*. What he discovered that whilst he spent some of this time wielding fantastic weapons and slaying dragons, much of the time was spent collecting herbs, trading goods, planning raids, joining guilds and understanding the social norms that underpin player interactions. Managing resources, forming teams, planning and working out the local politics sounds remarkably like a day in the office, even if we don't usually wear chainmail and wield battle axes. Stenberger describes spending a whole day gathering materials to manufacture a sword or a pair of special shoes not for the benefit of the individual player, but for the team involved in a raid against Azeroth's most fearsome of creatures. Selfless labour for the benefit of the group should resonate with anyone who has played their part by working hard on their aspect of a wider project.

Serious Fun

Jane McGonigal, in a notable TED Talk, 'Gaming Can Make a Better World', observed that the average *World of Warcraft* player plays an average of 22 hours per week. This is only slightly less than the midpoint between 16 and 32 hours, which is the US definition of a part-time worker. *WoW* players do this voluntarily, and usually in addition to, not instead of, their working week. This often provokes the reaction, 'How sad.' We shake our head in disbelief that the world is crumbling around us whilst gamers sit in darkened rooms, the only colour in their pallid complexions the reflected glow of a monitor playing out the vivid world of Azeroth in their bedrooms. McGonigal doesn't really help their case with the numbers either. According to her research, by the age of 21, the average American has spent 10,000 hours playing computer and video games. This is roughly the same amount of time they will spend in the classroom from fifth grade to graduating from high school (usually the fifth year after kindergarten until age 18), assuming their attendance is near perfect. Ten thousand hours is significant for another reason, too.

According to Malcolm Gladwell in his best-selling book *Outliers*, 10,000 hours is literally the point at which practice makes perfect. What Gladwell discovered was that those who had reached the top of their field had consistently invested 10,000 hours to do so. This level of investment in effort took them from a point where they were simply good at something to the point where they were concert-standard, virtuoso, exceptional. They became outliers.

It's tempting to assume that those born since the 1990s are going to excel at precisely the wrong things. Parents should be deeply concerned about it. At least they would be if they hadn't spent so much time being passively rather than interactively entertained themselves. Assuming they were born in the 1960s, these parents have spent 50,000 hours watching television. Clay Shirky, author of *Here Comes Everybody*, calls this, in his book of the same name, the *Cognitive Surplus*. Watching *Fantasy Island* and *The Love Boat* was a part-time job for post-war, industrialised baby boomers. So before wagging the finger of condemnation at our teenagers and 20-year-olds, we should reflect that we have spent a full five years of the last forty to fifty observing familiar characters in a bar where everybody knows their name. It really doesn't matter whether the intellectual and moral high ground is built on a foundation of *Hill Street Blues* and *Miami Vice* or *Panorama* and *The South Bank Show*. It's not particularly sturdy.

Fun for Free

We also assume that fun is self-motivating. We're intrinsically motivated to participate rather than requiring incentives. Unless we're professionals, we don't demand payment for time on a tennis court. Nor do we expect a cash reward for time spent in front of a video console or around a boardgame. We work for pay, but we play freely. However, it's not that simple. Play can be no fun at all, at least for some. For many, golf is 'a good walked spoiled' – a sentiment variously ascribed to Mark Twain, William Gladstone and others by golf widows and widowers the world over. Many will hoot in derision at the amount of time their friends play *World of Warcraft*, then settle down in a sun lounger on a two-week vacation with nothing more stimulating than a book or two of sudoku puzzles. Others don't see the appeal of completing a 9 × 9 grid so that each row, column and 3 × 3 sub-grid contains all of the digits from 1 to 9. Peter Norvig, a Director of Research at Google, was so bemused by his wife's interest in sudoku that he wrote a program to solve them. He believed, somewhat erroneously as it turns out, that if he could demonstrate that the computer could programmatically solve them, then she need spend no more time on them.

Bernard Suits, in his book *The Grasshopper: Games of Life and Utopia*, defines playing a game as 'the voluntary attempt to overcome unnecessary obstacles'. This definition is a crisp explanation of video games, geocaching, chess and *Othello* (a moment to learn, a lifetime to master). It also explains *SimCity* and *FarmVille*, which might otherwise be thought of as town planning or rural servitude. It's the only logical explanation for the game of golf. As McGonigal observes, it makes no sense on the surface. We try to get a small ball in a slightly larger hole by hitting it with a long and clumsy stick across hazards that include long grass, trees, bunkers and ponds. Objectively, we should be walking to the short grass and 'dropping the ball in the damned hole'. However, we don't. Indeed, it's our willingness not to take the easy route that makes it so much fun.

Easy and Hard Fun

So no single activity is fun for everyone. What is fun to one may be laborious to others. It might literally require an attitude of long and arduous work. If some forms of fun, for some people, are not really fun at all, then it opens up the possibility that some forms of work, for some people, can absolutely be fun. It might not be the instinctive easy-going fun we first think of, it might be something which is sometimes referred to as 'hard fun'.

Nicole Lazzaro, founder of XEODesign, a consultancy serving some of the most well-known video game producers such as Electronic Arts, Maxis and Ubisoft, has built a framework which describes the spectrum of emotions associated with fun. Lazzaro has identified that whilst some forms of fun are easy, others can be difficult without losing any of their intrinsic joy. Lazzaro conducted a number of studies in building the framework, one of which used facial action coding. This system, used by American psychologist Paul Ekman, whose work inspired the television series *Lie to Me*, captures facial expressions and systematically categorises them as determinations of emotion. Using this research, Lazzaro is able to explain the enduring effects of games such as *Angry Birds* and *Fruit Ninja*. She has also been able to help us understand fun in more detail with her landmark research piece 'The 4 Keys 2 Fun'.

The first key, unsurprisingly, is *easy fun*. Easy fun is about novelty, distraction and curiosity. It's about what hooks us into a game. Easy fun is the closest of the four keys to the common notion of fun, and the emotions frequently associated with easy fun include surprise and wonder.

Easy fun is rarely enough for all but the most easily distracted, so it isn't long before there's a need for a little more challenge, in what Lazzaro refers to as simply *hard fun*. Hard fun is about challenges, goals, achievement and mastery. Players need to overcome obstacles, pursue goals, test skills and feel a sense of accomplishment. Hard fun is already starting to sound a little less like fun in its purest sense, and more like work. Best practice in constructing a curriculum vitae or résumé, for example, is to build it around achievements. There would also be a separate section for skills. Every year, a manager will discuss, set and document goals with each of their team in an annual appraisal process. The emotions most associated with this key are frustration with difficult situations, and triumph in overcoming them. In fact, the ultimate gaming emotion is *fiero*. *Fiero*, the Italian word for 'pride', is the elation after a significant discovery or a hard-won successful outcome. *Fiero* is universally expressed by players throwing up their arms over their heads and in the air.

The third key, *altered states*, involves players moving from one state of mind to another. This is often thought of as 'games as therapy'. Players are looking to clear their heads through immersive play, or they may just be trying to avoid boredom. There are times when we experience this in the workplace. It's what Hungarian psychology professor Mihály Csíkszentmihályi refers to in his book *Flow: The Psychology of Optimal Experience*. Csíkszentmihályi, notable for his work in the study of creativity and happiness, would characterise flow as focused motivation accompanied by feelings of joy whilst performing the task.

The final key to fun is what Lazzaro refers to as *the people factor*. This is the social aspect of fun, which is often overlooked by parents who mistakenly think of video gaming as a strictly solo activity. However, there's as much teamwork and camaraderie in a game of *Call of Duty* as there is in a game of football. Banter and bad language that teeter between healthy rivalry and abuse are common in both, in my experience. Players who use this key are often treating the game as a vehicle for socialising. This can be co-operative gaming, or comparing notes about their progress with their group later. Surprisingly, there are many who play games who may otherwise not like to spend time with their friends. Two emotions related to the people factor that are worthy of note are *naches* and *Schadenfreude*.

Many of us are familiar with schadenfreude, an English word borrowed from German, derived from *Schaden*, meaning harm, and *Freude*, meaning joy. As the puppets in the West End musical *Avenue Q* suggest in a song called 'Schadenfreude': 'it makes me glad I am not you'. The lesser-known *naches* or *kvell* are Yiddish terms. They describe the pride and the pleasure at observing the achievements of a child or mentee. It goes beyond being a proud Jewish parent, though. It was common in my own home for my son and his friends to play games together in a way that I couldn't explain until I heard Lazzaro talk about *naches*. They would mostly play games co-operatively or in competition, either in split-screen mode in the same room or on their own consoles but connected online. Occasionally, though, only one of them would play a game, whilst the other watched. Surprisingly, to me at least, both appeared to be enjoying the experience. On occasions, I would offer a mild suggestion to 'let your friend have a go', but neither seemed concerned. I let it go, assuming that my son's friends, more than capable of asserting their own opinion, would sort it out without parental intervention. However, the notion of *naches* explains why they seemed sanguine. Sometimes players can take their emotions vicariously. Like a mother or mentor, gamers can get wrapped up in the achievements of their friends.

Mission Roundup

In the first two chapters, we examined how our behaviours as consumers and producers can't be completely explained through economic theory alone. The reasons why we bristle against being defined in economic terms are the very same reasons why these terms are inadequate.

In this chapter, we have also challenged the nature of work and fun. Fun is not limited by notions of being easy and distracting. Indeed, it can be difficult and complex, involving strenuous activity. Yet we find it rewarding, satisfying and engaging, to the point where we may take part without financial inducement. It's activity that we find rewarding and engaging for its own sake. Lazzaro's work on understanding the nature of fun reveals much about player emotions, and it's not all about escapism or switching off. These emotions, captured as visceral responses, can certainly involve excitement and wonder. However, they can also be about resolving difficult challenges, immersive activity and social experiences of teamwork, competition and collaboration. These emotions, whilst observed during game play, are far from being exclusive to gaming. What lies here, in the blurred lines between fun and work, is the subject of the subsequent chapters in *World of Workcraft*.

Chapter 4
The Grindstone

The Game

Knowledge workers, first described by Peter Drucker in his 1959 book *The Landmarks of Tomorrow*, enjoy more mentally challenging work than primary workers such as miners, fishermen and farmers, who are subject to more physical demands. However, much of what's undertaken by technicians, managers and sales representatives is routine, some of it dull. Even the most stimulating jobs involve a modicum of drudgery. There's little we can do to motivate ourselves or others to do these things. They just need to be done. After all, we get paid to work, to do our jobs, and that includes those elements that don't require much of a challenge. Games, on the other hand, allow us to escape the tedium of today through a future of galactic battles or a mythical past of dragon slaying. In these realms, reality is replaced with fantasy, the daily grind with exhilaration, the nuance and complexity of life with a quick and easy video game fix. In fact, this is why gamers game. In space, no one can hear you scream, nor can they hear the quiet hum of industry or the occasional sigh of boredom. Even if we accept that fun can be difficult and challenging, it's never uninteresting. It's never like real life. No one would, in the manner of a fourteenth-century knife sharpener bending over their work, put their nose to the grindstone for fun. Or would they?

The Badges

- Graft Graduate

- Game Mechanic

- Behavioural Beginner

- True Motivator

Graft

After graduating in 1995, Eran Egozy and Alex Rigopulos launched a music
and technology business, Harmonix, with $100,000 raised from their friends
and family. Their first product, *The Axe*, was a music improvisation system
using only a joystick. The product made an amazing demonstration. The
experience was, by all accounts, almost magical, and the pair took every
opportunity to share their creation. But players lost interest quickly and
The Axe was ultimately, by their own admission, a horrendous failure, having
sold just 300 copies. This led to a deal with Disney, though, and the technology,
now controlled by infrared hand-tracking sensors instead of a joystick, found
itself inside an Epcot Center science and technology exhibit. Whilst adding the
prestigious Disney name to their list of clients earned them kudos, it didn't
net their business much in terms of long-term profitability, so they turned to
the Japanese karaoke business. After a long, hard eighteen months, the pair
admitted defeat. Their product, about musical expression, flopped in a difficult
and foreign market that was about people reproducing music, not improvising
around it. They retreated, reconsidered and made some difficult decisions,
including letting staff go, as they tried to conserve what little cash they had left.
After five years, almost zero revenues and repeated failures, they released their
first moderately successful game, *Frequency*. They followed up with another
success, *Karaoke Revolution*, before transforming the video game industry with
the blockbuster *Rock Band*. By 2011, the *Rock Band* franchise had become one
of the five highest-grossing video games, generating in excess of $600,000,000.

The story behind many successes like *Rock Band* is similar. Overnight
success only looks overnight from a distance. In fact, high attainment in any
field is usually the result of persistence and hard work. The band headlining
at Glastonbury most likely played small halls and bars in out-of-the-way
places for a decade. The medal-adorned athlete might be picking up accolades
and sponsorship deals today, but check her alarm clock and it's most likely
permanently set at 5 a.m. The Vice President of Sales no doubt served her time
as a rep, too. There may have been a time where she was only allowed back
into her office at the end of the day, when she had a briefcase full of headed
notepaper to prove to her boss that she had visited every single business in
an office park. That notepaper – evidence that she had demonstrated their
new photocopier model to each and every office manager – was the minimum
required to keep her job. Achieving anything requires effort. It invites failure
and difficulties that must be overcome. Chance plays its part in all we do, but
the reality is that there are few shortcuts to success. And it isn't just long-term
business success and lifelong careers that require hard work. Each point

along the way, each minor victory and cause for celebration, is just the same. A completed project, a successful meeting, a well-crafted document are all preceded by effort, by graft. And often lots of it.

A common reaction to gamification is that gamers prefer the world of gaming precisely because it's not like this. Games remove the need for prolonged preparation and chores. The learning curve is short, if there's a learning curve at all. In previous chapters, we began to challenge this. Nicole Lazzaro's work on the subject of fun illustrates that whilst we instinctively think of fun as easy and relaxing, it can also be challenging, and sometimes hard work.

Grind

So games can be difficult, yet rewarding. They can, according to Lazzaro, be 'hard fun' – and all the more enjoyable for being so. This, in many ways, isn't hard to believe. The fun's in the challenge. However, games can also be engagingly uninteresting. Like life, there can be prolonged periods of tedium. Gamers will, without payment, indulge in monotony that most would otherwise require salaries, payment or other incentives to carry out. In fact, gamers have a name for it. They call it 'grinding'.

Grinding, also called 'treadmilling', describes gaming activity that's repetitive or, in itself, uninteresting and uninspiring. It's most common in massively multiplayer online role-playing games (MMORPGs), and in older MMORPGs it was the primary way gamers could advance their characters' levels. However, designers of contemporary MMORPGs are being challenged to reimagine grind for increasingly sophisticated players. Those who don't are departing from believable narrative. They are, ironically, making the game less realistic. For example, in an early version of the MMORPG *Star Wars Galaxies*, one character could deliberately self-inflict minor injuries to allow a second to rapidly improve their healing ability by repeatedly treating the first player. Eventually, the experience mechanics had to be overhauled and updated so that grinding, in itself, wasn't enough. Grinding is often a means to an end in a gaming experience. Experience requires putting in the hours, building up virtual currency requires extended periods of waiting and saving, amassing resources requires long days of farming. This is considerably more like real life than those who don't game or don't scrutinise what gamers are really doing might imagine.

Grind doesn't just appear in role-playing games. Much of the phenomenally successful game *FarmVille*, from social game provider Zynga, could be described as agricultural drudgery. The game was one of the first to make use of a game mechanic referred to as *the appointment dynamic.* This mechanic, in many ways, couldn't be more tiresome. Having planted virtual crops, the player must return within a certain period to harvest them. Those who miss their appointment are faced with withered crops and have to begin planting again. *SimCity BuildIt* uses the same mechanic. Players that don't return to attend to cargo ships will miss opportunities to trade. They literally miss the boat. The appointment mechanic is the video game equivalent of remembering to take medication or collecting dry cleaning. It's virtual routine, digital drudgery.

Tasks, Activities, Work and Play

In their book *Total Engagement,* Byron Reeves and J. Leighton Read systematically analyse gaming activities, comparing them with work and assessing their similarities. Reeves, a professor in the Department of Communication at Stanford, was able to recruit students to analyse the detail of their gaming activity, but the exercise also required a rigorous understanding of the basic tasks and activities that work is comprised of.

To do this, they utilised a database of activities published by the Occupational Information Network (O*Net), a US Department of Labor-sponsored project. O*Net is a large-scale collaboration with the North Carolina Employment Security Commission which publishes and maintains data on over 800 occupations and provides tools and resources to help businesses design jobs and match candidates' skills to roles. Specifically, the team used a list of O*Net generalised work activities that covered all of the key building blocks of modern work – for example, 'Monitor Processes, Materials, or Surroundings – Monitoring and reviewing information from materials, events, or the environment to detect or assess problems'.

For each of the work activities, the team identified gamer experiences. As an example, the team asked gamers to match their game experiences to the following work activity: 'Getting Information – observing, receiving, and otherwise obtaining information from all relevant sources'. They immediately identified matching gamer experiences. In THQ's game *Company of Heroes,* players scout the opposing party using a swift squad of infantry to see which units their opponent is upgrading. It's a reasonable example of grinding. It's not, in itself, a thrilling activity in a game full of simulated skirmishes and battles, but it's a common device in real-time strategy games. It's a means to an end, a distraction from core business, but an activity that will inform tactics and strategies. This is identical to many information-gathering exercises in any business. Analytics, business intelligence and reporting are routine information-gathering exercises to inform the next monthly, quarterly or annual business cycle.

Information gathering in gaming can extend well beyond the game itself. In *World of Warcraft*, prior to the first attempt at defeating a 'boss', all members of a guild are expected to make themselves aware of information about how the boss might attack and the role they will play as an individual in the attack. To do this, each player will check the *World of Warcraft* wiki.[1] The wiki, which provides information on quests, items and the *Warcraft* universe, is the second-largest English-language wiki in the world, only ranking behind Wikipedia itself, with 3 million unique users each month.

The team diligently worked through a taxonomy intended to cover all the key building blocks of modern jobs in this way. They analysed and understood generalised work activities, and researched games to look for examples. Reeves and Read expected to find a reasonable volume of gamer activity that could be matched to work activity. However, their findings surprised them. It wasn't the fact that there was overlap between the O*Net list and gamer experiences, it was the fact that *every* skill in the O*Net list could be represented several times over in gamer experiences.

People are frequently and freely engaging in activity that businesses pay workers to do. More than this, they're paying games publishers for the privilege. Of course, there's some subjectivity in the comparison, and there are other equally serious work classification systems. However, this takes us a long way away from the default and somewhat lazy view that all gaming activity is fun, and all working activity isn't. It demonstrates, at the very least, that most activity we would regard as work has been designed into a gaming experience, and that the designers have done so in such a way as to make that work compelling, interesting and engaging.

Motivation, Ability, Activation

At the heart of our assertion that gaming activity can be hard work that requires no payment, compensation or reward is the field of human behaviour. Indeed, at the core of gamification is the idea that human behaviour can be influenced

---

1   www.wowwiki.com.

through digital design. One pioneer in this field is Professor B.J. Fogg, who runs the Persuasive Technology Lab at Stanford University. As a doctoral student at Stanford, Fogg used experimental psychology to demonstrate that computers can be used to predictably change human behaviours. As part of his work, he developed a behavioural model which suggests that for a person to perform any behaviour, they must be sufficiently motivated, must have the ability to perform the behaviour, and must be triggered in some way to do so. The importance of this work lies not in the identification of the three factors (motivation, ability and trigger), but that they must be present in the same moment for the behaviour to occur. As with stand-up comedy, timing is everything. In fact, the ancient Greeks had a word for it – *kairos*, the opportune moment to persuade.

The Fogg Behavior Model includes the notion of an activation threshold. When an individual has sufficient ability and motivation, then a trigger will lead to the target behaviour. A trigger when that individual is outside the threshold will fail. It will annoy or distract. Spam email is a trigger, but rarely finds us when we're motivated to respond. In fact, the source of our dissatisfaction with email more generally is that it's a trigger that's poorly aligned to ability. Ability, in the broader sense, relates not just to skill, but to time, attention, mental capacity and any other resources required to fulfil the behaviour. An email arrives at a time suited to the sender, not the recipient. Email rarely arrives when we're at the activation threshold. Instead, it arrives as an unfulfilled obligation, and instead becomes a minor, or sometimes major, source of stress for many.

Much of what has been done in the entire field of enterprise systems design to date has been related to ability. Tasks that take too long or require a long list of operations are simplified to bring them into the normal range of an individual's abilities. Dr Michael Wu, Chief Scientist for social software vendor Lithium, describes an alternative approach in his blog post 'The Magic Potion of Game Dynamics'. Instead of making the target behaviour simple, systems can make it *appear* simpler through a three-step process:

1. **Divide and Conquer** – Break the target behaviour down into simpler and smaller tasks.

2. **Cognitive Rehearsal** – Demonstrate how straightforward the behaviour really is.

3. **Cascading Information** – Provide just enough information for each stage of the activity.

There are also delicate tradeoffs between motivation and ability. We are most highly motivated when the activity is challenging, but not so difficult as to cause us anxiety, and simple enough to achieve, but not to the point of being repetitive or uninteresting. This is how we achieve what Mihály Csíkszentmihályi refers to as *flow*. Whilst video games typically adapt as our skills improve, to keep us in a state of flow, enterprise systems are designed to reduce tasks to their simplest and most manageable level. They then rarely adapt themselves, except in the most basic ways, to the human capacity for continuous learning.

This still leaves two of Fogg's factors largely untouched. Triggers certainly exist, in the form of prompts, messages and alerts, but motivation is rarely a consideration for enterprise systems design. Even if it was a consideration, most business analysts, solution architects or systems designers would rationalise that their system will be used by salaried employees, so their motivations are a given.

Missed Motivation

We've touched on motivation in previous chapters, largely to challenge the notion that only carrots and sticks can move us into Fogg's activation threshold. Daniel Pink, in his book *Drive: The Surprising Truth about What Motivates Us*, draws on decades of scientific research into human motivation and identifies that performance is poorly correlated to money. One of these studies, 'Large Stakes and Big Mistakes', conducted by four professors including Dan Ariely and involving Massachusetts Institute of Technology (MIT), Carnegie Mellon and the University of Chicago, involved a large number of students performing a variety of tasks in return for rewards. One group were awarded small, one medium and one large cash incentives. For completely mechanical tasks, there was a strong correlation between reward and performance. This was no surprise. However, tasks that involved even the most rudimentary cognitive skill didn't follow the same pattern at all – in fact, the larger the reward, the poorer the performance. Top-tier economists from MIT, Carnegie Mellon and the University of Chicago reached a conclusion that flies in the face of the way most companies build their reward and performance management systems: higher rewards did not lead to better performance. What's more, they repeated the tests in rural India, where the monetary rewards were as high as two months' salary for the participants, with exactly the same results. The group offered the top reward performed the worst of all. It would appear that the influence of carrots and sticks on human motivation is highly questionable. Money is, of course, an important motivation – but only in so far as it needs to be 'enough'.

We can't be paid, it seems, to move into Fogg's activation threshold. Our motivation, according to Pink, comes from four things: purpose, mastery, autonomy and relatedness. We need to make a difference, we need to get better at doing it, we want to do it our own way, and we want to share with our friends and colleagues.

Mission Roundup

Sustainable success in all fields requires a significant amount of hard work. Stephen Covey, author of *The 7 Habits of Highly Effective People*, articulates this as: 'Private victories precede public victories.' He goes on to say: 'you cannot invert this process any more than you can harvest a crop before you plant it'. Those who regard gamers from a distance cite this as one of the most significant differences between gaming and 'the real world'. Gamers, they argue, are looking for the shortcut, they're looking to get to glory and victory without the practice. They're looking for results without application. Interestingly, though, success in many video games requires activity which, when analysed with some rigour, exhibits all the characteristics of what might traditionally be thought of as work. It's well-designed work, though. It's in the 'sweet spot' of ability and motivation, where we're not only receptive, but willing to be triggered to perform what otherwise might be thought of as ordinary and mundane tasks.

It isn't that games don't include work. They clearly do. The difference is that the work is well designed. The balance between ability and difficulty has been thoughtfully considered from every possible angle. Ultimately, the work has been designed to bring together motivation, ability and a reason to do it in a single moment.

Chapter 5
The Efficiency Paradox

The Game

The post-industrial age saw organisations optimising the tasks and activities that make up their business processes. New methodologies have been developed, designed and deployed in the name of efficiency. Disciplines such as Six Sigma have been adopted, sometimes with religious fervour, sweeping through departments and across divisions, driven by experts who are known as 'black belts'. Endless energy has been expended on eradicating erroneous labour. By any analysis, the absence of unnecessary work should have created a workplace where we're all highly motivated by sharply focused and purposeful activity, secure in the knowledge that everything we do is contributing to the goals of the business.

The reality, though, is somewhat different. The workforce in the Western world are thoroughly demotivated. The workplace has all but completely disengaged. What we do is optimal, but we don't do it optimally. A listless workforce, sleepwalking through hyper-optimised business processes, can't be good for any business. It manifestly can't serve the very objectives it sets out to achieve.

The impact of perfect processes, then, is unclear. Whilst little we do is wasted, something is still missing from the modern workplace. If not efficiency, what else will make us feel that our time is well spent?

The Badges

- Bartle Typer

- Efficiency Evangelist

- Penny Blossom

- Human Design

Game Design

Richard Bartle is a researcher and writer living in the cathedral city of Ripon in the north of England. Bartle was responsible for causing a chronic lack of sleep amongst pioneering gaming enthusiasts, including me, in the early 1980s. A student in Essex at the time, Bartle was the developer responsible for many of the puzzles in the first online virtual world multi-user dungeon (MUD). Players of the dungeon where given access to Essex University's Digital Equipment Corporation (DEC) computer over a British Telecom packet switch network at some considerable cost. The reward for the interminably slow speed and frequent disconnects was access to a world portrayed not in the glorious high-resolution graphics seen in games like *World of Warcraft* and *Eve*, but in simple narrative – that is to say, in text. Moving around the world required the use of commands like DROP, GET and GIVE. Those who were stuck could ask for a HINT. The user experience was all in glorious 80-column and 24-line monochrome, with nothing more graphically advanced than boxes drawn with asterisks.

Bartle is also a pioneer in putting people at the front and centre of games design. Before Bartle, early designers didn't consider individual motivations. Instead, the formative years in gaming relied on superficial advancements in the speed of play, the number of levels and the quality of graphics. In those early days, game designers had the advantage of working with gaming enthusiasts, and engagement was sometimes intuitive and sometimes accidental, rather than designed from the outset. Bartle changed this. He developed a paper in 1996 which was later expanded into the Bartle Test of Gamer Psychology. The test, a series of questions, categorises players into one of four characters by calculating their 'Bartle Quotient'. The questions include 'Is it better to be loved or feared?' and 'Would you rather [in a multiplayer online game] have a spell that increases the rate at which you gain experience points or a spell to damage other players?' The test has been taken more than 750,000 times on just one site for computer and video game players, gamerDNA.[1] The outcome is a personal classification across one of four player types: Achievers, Explorers, Socialisers and Killers.

---

1   www.gamerDNA.com.

Achievers are players motivated by gaining points, advancing levels and collecting new equipment. Achievers explore, but only to identify new sources of treasure. They kill too, although this is about removing their rivals or gaining the points that some games award for obliterating other characters. Faced with a game such as *Lego Lord of the Rings*, Achievers will spend evenings and weekends trying to reach 100 per cent completion and ensuring that they have all 80 playable characters or mini-figures.

Explorers are motivated by experiences. They hunt for interesting locations in out-of-the-way places. The 15-year-old boy who found the very first video game 'Easter egg' in the 1979 Atari video game *Adventure* was almost undoubtedly an Explorer. A hidden room containing the author's name was only visible once the player had found a single-pixel dot, itself difficult to locate, and placed it in a very specific part of the east end of one corridor in combination with a selection of other dots. The unlikely series of actions required to find Easter eggs are tenuously related to the overall objective of the game at best. In fact, their largely unnecessary nature is a giveaway for Explorers, who are chiefly motivated by discovery. They will also be able to retell their most memorable stint in the 1998 fantasy role-playing game *Baldur's Gate*, in narrative so well crafted that it will feel like they're sharing a chapter from a fantasy novel rather than their physical experiences with a controller and a screen.

For *Socialisers*, the game is a means to an end. They are drawn to online gaming because of the potential to connect with others. For them, it's about the interplay during and after the game. It's the opportunities to empathise, to chat and to engage in banter and 'trash talk' that keep Socialisers playing. In real life, Socialisers are often great networkers, motivated not just by the size, but also the quality of their network.

Killers socialise, but they are, to quote Bartle, people of few words. Their socialising is chiefly about taunting and gloating. They are driven by a strong competitive spirit, and enjoy the sporting nature of gaming, pitting their skills against those of others. Mostly, though, Killers like winning, they like being the first to a high score or the last man or woman standing. Bartle suggests that 'killers get their kicks from imposing themselves on others', and goes on to suggest that 'the more massive the distress caused, the greater the killer's joy at having caused it'. The first- and third-person shooter franchise *Call of Duty* is a natural home for Killers. The simulated warfare is a perfect environment to allow them to run riot with virtual machine guns, flamethrowers and grenades.

Bartle's player types were only the beginning. What Bartle started was a whole new body of work on player psychology provoking many new models none of which take player motivation for granted.

Business Systems Design

Business systems are also subject to deliberate design disciplines. In fact, intuitively, we would think of these as more scientific, more professional and more thorough than those behind games. Systems design approaches have changed radically over their recent history. Approaches in the 1980s were methodical, step-by-step and formal. Each phase typically required signatures from all involved parties or stakeholders before the next phase could be started. This was known as 'waterfall', its primary purpose being to control the enormous costs associated with large software projects. Development activity couldn't begin until the design phase was ratified by a project steering committee. The design phase couldn't start until the analysis stage was documented and agreed, and so on. The next decade introduced more iterative approaches, such as dynamic systems design or rapid application development, essentially built on the premise that no one really knows exactly what their requirement is until they see it. Unlike previous waterfall approaches, these allowed business users and designers to collaborate and iterate around a design until requirements became much more clearly understood.

At around the same time as the widespread adoption of dynamic systems design, a closely related discipline, business process re-engineering, was being pioneered. It focused on the analysis of processes within an organisation – usually, but not always, as an input into systems design. Business activities were scrutinised, analysed and optimised spurred on by analysis such as the 2004 Gartner report *Justifying BPM Projects* which reported that 78 per cent of business process management projects saw an internal rate of return of 15 per cent or more.

At its height, more than half of major global corporates had either re-engineered or had plans to do so. Major transformation programmes costing millions of dollars transformed the business of work, often as part of software automation implementing enterprise resource planning systems. Their purpose was to improve speed and efficiency. Waste and redundancy, in the form of needless, duplicate or error-prone activity, was hunted down and driven out of town. If a process didn't add obvious value, its days were numbered. Other approaches, such as total quality management, were designed to achieve the same results, but through a series of small, continuous improvements rather than large-scale, disruptive and dramatic redesign. Typically, these initiatives were conducted with major consultancy firms that had experience in employing these approaches with other companies and offered advantages associated with an external perspective.

Business re-engineering programmes are alive and well today as a service offering from any of the large consultancy firms, including Accenture, Deloitte, Capgemini, Ernst & Young and IBM Global Business Services. As an example, Deloitte advertises on its corporate home page that it will 'help organisations by revealing problems, bottlenecks and inefficiencies in a permanent and structured way, in order to reduce lead times, decrease costs, improve internal efficiency and qualitative and quantitative outcomes'.

Making Better Work, or Making Work Better

This level of investment in the design of systems and processes often leads to more work being achieved with less effort. It means that mistakes are minimised, and when they do occur, they're dealt with quickly. We all react well to this. Few of us relish being involved in work that's inefficient, or worse, pointless. And when things do go wrong, we want to be supported in such a way that we can resolve problems quickly without too much conflict. We know when work is unimportant or inefficient, and it's no fun. However, efficiency in and of itself is not motivating.

This is illustrated by an episode of the CBS television comedy *The Big Bang Theory* called 'The Work Song Nanocluster'. The character Penny develops a home-made hair clip called a 'Penny Blossom', which she plans to develop into a profitable home-based business. Sheldon Cooper, her socially inept and borderline autistic neighbour, played by Jim Parsons, points out that her plan isn't viable without a dramatic improvement in her production process. As the story develops, she implements a production line with the help of Sheldon, his roommate, Leonard Hofstadter, and other characters from the show. Slowly, the dream of independence, self-sufficiency and rewarding work is replaced by rapid but repetitive processes that require singing sea shanties to keep everyone motivated. Slowly, aspiration and joy are replaced with the mundanity of sticking and pasting. Whilst it's played for comedic effect, it's a surprisingly accurate allegory of the decline from purposeful industry to dispiriting efficiency. What it illustrates is an inherent conflict of interests. As an individual, Penny was perhaps motivated by the satisfaction of creating a quality, handcrafted accessory, each one unique. The economic realities, once some basic market assumptions about price and sales volume had been established, required them to be made quickly and cheaply. The structural needs of the business were not aligned to the needs of Penny as an individual or agent. Sociologists refer to this as agency versus structure.

It would seem that human motivation is not contemplated in business process design. When it is referred to, it's typically in the context of change management. Out of the millions of words written on this subject, most of them are focused on how to deal with reluctant staff, uncomfortable with change or with a vested interest in the status quo. The primary consideration is how to gain buy-in from those resistant to change or unable to see the bigger picture, so that the project can proceed unhindered.

Figure 5.1   Agile Manifesto

Source: Creative Commons, visualpun.ch, 'Agile Manifesto'. https://creativecommons.org/licenses/by-sa/2.0/.

The needs of individuals, even in contemporary systems design methods is still playing catch-up. One such approach – actually, a whole movement – originated in 2001 when a group of software developers met in a ski resort in Utah. Frustrated with heavyweight, slow and cumbersome project approaches, their ambition was to create something more lightweight and agile. They established a set of principles, referred to as 'The Agile Manifesto', one of which was that individuals and interactions should be a primary consideration. Whilst this acknowledges the importance of people, it is, strictly speaking, referring to the development process and the project team, rather than the systems they're building or the people they're for.

More recently, though, there has been a proliferation of corporate systems built for use by customers, driven chiefly by mobile and electronic commerce. For the first time, enterprise software was being designed to be used by volunteers rather than a salaried workforce. Design considerations had to go beyond concepts of pure functionality and usability – the traditional concerns of systems design and human–computer interaction. Instead, concepts that are difficult to define, such as attractiveness, fun or consistency with the brand proposition, became design goals. The field of user experience emerged – an interdisciplinary field, borrowing from industrial design, visual design, software engineering and psychology, amongst others. The term is widely adopted, but there's no meaningful consensus on what it is. Marc Hassenzahl, Professor for Experience and Interaction at the Folkwang University of the Arts in Essen, has built a highly regarded model originally set out in the International Journal of Human-Computer Interaction in 2001. He divides the user experience across two dimensions. The first is *pragmatic qualities*, which focuses on attributes like 'clarity', 'supporting' and 'useful' – all comparable to traditional notions of functionality. Secondly, Hassenzahl considers *hedonic qualities*, which have little to do with utility, and everything to do with delight and pleasure. These attributes include 'interesting', 'exciting' and 'impressive'. These two dimensions are independent of one another, which bears out our experience of enterprise software, which is generally usable, but not appealing. Of course, it also follows that some interactive software can be appealing, but not terribly useful.

User experience design is in its infancy, and is for the most part employed in systems for customers rather than internal systems, which continue to be designed for efficiency. When systems are not efficient, executives bring in external expertise to 'reduce lead times, decrease costs, improve internal efficiency and qualitative and quantitative outcome' by implementing new ones. They are not, however, designed for the people who run them. The hearts and minds of employees are somewhat taken for granted, and the data back this up.

Working the Work

The state of work then would appear to be optimal. However the state of the workforce is anything but. Almost two-thirds of employees are either not engaged or are actively disengaged. In other words, the individuals who have responsibility for optimised business activities are emotionally disconnected from them.

Two Towers Watson (formerly Towers Perrin) Global Workforce studies in 2012 and 2014 and a Gallup report *The State of the American Workplace* published in 2013 all conclude that only around a third of the workforce are engaged.

The Towers Watson 2014 study gathered responses from 32,000 respondents in 26 countries; the Gallup study conducted its research on the US working population via its Gallup Panel, with sample sizes ranging from 2,192 to 151,290 full- and part-time workers. The weight of evidence is irrefutable. Process design, systems, working practices and management models are not connecting us to the work we do. Gallup, identified three levels of engagement. The first was *engaged employees*. These employees work with passion, and they feel a profound connection with their company. They are the individuals most likely to innovate and move the business forward in what is a time of change. The second was *unengaged employees*. These individuals are listlessly marking time until they can physically check out, having spent much of their working day emotionally checked out anyway. The final, and most worrying, category is *actively disengaged employees*. These are not just unhappy, they are also undermining what their engaged co-workers are achieving. Only a third are engaged. The remaining two thirds are not and some are bringing everyone down.

In summary, process improvement is bringing about positive change. The most visible improvements will be where there's little human interaction and the improvements are systems-centred. Where there are people involved, though, it's a different matter. The numbers have been pretty much consistent for the last decade. Almost a third of employees are engaged, half are not, and around a fifth are so disengaged that they monopolise their managers' time, account for more quality problems and spend more time off sick. All the good work being done by 30 per cent of the workforce is being undermined. This is the cost of ignoring motivation when we design work. Games acknowledge many player types but there is little if any consideration to basic human psychology in the engineering of processes.

Designing for People

Bartle was not the only game designer to create a classification of player types. In fact, the gamer types were somewhat specific to a specific genre of game: multi-user dungeons, the precursor to games like *World of Warcraft*. However, Bartle raised awareness that different people indulge in the same activity for different reasons. People, Bartle was essentially saying, are different. Social game designer Amy Jo Kim developed a similar model based on social engagement verbs and the motivational patterns that she observed in modern social gaming. Her model comprises four categories: *Compete, Collaborate, Explore* and *Express*. The first three approximate to Bartle's Achiever, Socialiser and Explorer. The fourth, a replacement for Bartle's Killer, is specific to social platforms and social gaming. Self-expression, Kim asserts, is a key driver for participants in social platforms. They are motivated by increasing their abilities to showcase their creativity and express who they are. In the world of social, there are those who observe, consume and read. Then there are those who create articles, blogs and videos and originate memes. These are demonstrating Express.

Another model originates from UK-based social media and gamification commentator Andrzej Marczewski. Marczewski proposes a separate set of player types, broken down into those who are intrinsically and those who are extrinsically motivated. In fact, he places them in a set of four yin/yang pairings: *Socialisers/Networkers, Free Spirits/Exploiters, Achievers/Consumers*, and finally, *Philanthropists/Self-seekers*. Whilst at first glance these can seem like a list of positive and negative personality traits, Marczewski makes the point that we are typically designing complex systems that require a mix of interdependent motivations in order for the system to function.

Socialisers are motivated by interacting and connecting with people, Networkers are more motivated by the social status of being well connected or by the advantages and favours they may be able to gain from their connections. Free Spirits are motivated by discovery, whilst Exploiters are looking for loopholes. Achievers are motivated by self-improvement or mastery, whilst Consumers are concerned with their status as a gold or platinum card holder. Finally, Philanthropists find their motivation in helping others, whilst Self-seekers are seeking to increase their status or earn points.

Mission Roundup

Accounting software is an unlikely place to find design inspiration. However, Philip Fierlinger, head of design at accounting software company Xero, describes his organisation as a user experience, not a software company. There are few things are more tedious than reconciling the company bank account, but Fierlinger designed Xero's solution after watching his three-year-old play a card matching game. The result is that users love reconciling in Xero.

There are other software solutions that are championing the cause of software that's pleasing, if not fun to use. *Expensify*, for example, is marketed as 'Expense reports that don't suck!' However, more than two decades after Bartle, business systems are still really playing catch-up. Whilst thought leaders like Kim and Marczewski refine the discussion about player motivation, the designers of mainstream enterprise software such as Oracle and Microsoft, and even modern platforms like Salesforce, barely acknowledge different user types, let alone design a user experience that will motivate and delight them.

And there's the paradox. Business processes and systems have been designed to be efficient, but without any consideration for the people that run them. The result is efficient processes, running inefficiently.

Chapter 6

All the World's a Game
(and all the Men and
Women Merely Players)

The Game

In 2012, the global gaming business was worth around $80 billion – about two-thirds of the global movie production and distribution business of $126 billion. The video game industry has had as significant a cultural impact on a whole generation as *Citizen Kane*, *The Elephant Man* and *Bambi* had on the generation before them. Cultural sensibilities are being gently shaped by new norms. Video games continue to be inspired by Hollywood properties like *Ghostbusters*, *Batman* and *Star Trek*. In turn, Hollywood has produced movies inspired by video games such as *Silent Hill*, *Max Payne* and *Hitman* – though, in truth, to very little critical acclaim. Art is inspiring life, life is inspiring art, and art is even inspiring art.

It was inevitable, then, that the rapidly emerging gaming world would overspill into other areas of society. An industry with such significant sway, with the power to engage us and absorb so much of our leisure time, must understand our motivations far more than we might superficially imagine. But the video game market has been around since at least the 1970s, with the introduction of the game *Pong*, so why, given decades of unrelenting growth, are we only just beginning to find so many uses for game techniques outside of video games? Why now?

The Badges

- Fitcoiner

- Mobile Worker

- Wearable Wonder

- Digital Native

Fuel the World

Global growth for the athletic footwear market between 2012 and 2016 was estimated to be 1.75 per cent according to the US analyst firm Research and Markets. During the same time Nike's estimated market share was expected to grow from 18.6 per cent to 22.8 per cent according to online statistics portal Statista. Its success is grounded in continuous innovation. *Fast Company* magazine named Nike the number one most innovative company in 2013, the same year the sportswear manufacturer recorded sales of $25 billion. In a 2014 *Financial Times* article, a spokesperson outlined why Nike+ Fuel was an important part of this innovation and core to their business. Nike+ Fuel is a universal points system that tracks personal activity originally on their own wearable device the Fuelband and on smartphones. Nike and their fuel system were also one of the original partners at the launch of the Apple watch in 2015.

It doesn't matter if you are playing football in Dorking, dodgeball in Hollywood or running in Chile. If you are tracking with Nike, Fuel+ points are universal. New possibilities are emerging as a result of such forward thinking. Austin-based creative designers, Chaotic Moon Studios, introduced a similar concept in the form of a 'fitcoin' in 2015 which they hoped would help businesses offer lower insurance rates, sportswear discounts or even be used as an online currency.

Heal the World

Chris Hewett was Executive Producer at Monolith Productions, an industry leader in cinematic games, when it released a whole stream of successful titles based on Hollywood movies that included *TRON* and *Alien vs. Predator*. His undoubted success, like many executives, came at a personal cost not least of which was his eighty-hour work week. Everything, according to Hewett, in an interview with Jesse Lahey host of the *Engaging Leader* management podcasts, was out of balance. Whilst his career was in great shape, nothing else was. The unrelenting focus on his work had left his relationships, his health and his sense of well-being at an all-time low. He threw himself into the business of reversing what had become a downward spiral. He searched, read, researched. He took counsel where he could, and whilst much of what he heard wasn't new and very little of it genuinely remarkable, the results were. He followed through with commitment, applying a series of life-affirming principles to each and every day, and transformed his life. Inspired by his own journey of self-help, he recognised that there was an opportunity to help others through gamified applications or digital interventions. The result was his company Mindbloom and an initial pair of life-transforming games *Life Game* and *Bloom*. *Life Game* uses a tree metaphor to visualise personal well-being. Players begin with nothing more than a stick and a few leaves. Recording actions such as drinking water, exercising, listening to music and getting enough sleep encourage the tree to grow and blossom. *Bloom* sends gentle reminders throughout the day to encourage users to follow through on their commitments to practise guitar, call their parents or let go of grudges. Each reminder, or bloom, is a beautifully presented movie or set of images. Mindbloom products have evidently tapped into a yearning for better lifestyles. *Bloom* alone has been downloaded more than a quarter of a million times.

Wearable World

Those who monitor and measure their physical activity with Nike+ Fuel or their emotional and spiritual growth encouraged by inspirational blooms owe a debt to Mark Weiser. Weiser, a researcher at Xerox's PARC (Palo Alto Research Center), predicted the very devices that would make Nike+ Fuel and *Life Game* possible in 1991 when he published the article 'The Computer for the 21st Century' in *Scientific American* magazine. Weiser imaginatively wrapped a story around 'Sal', a professional single mother to illustrate how computers had evolved around her needs not the other way around. In the post-personal computer (PC) world ambient, context aware and ubiquitous devices made Sal's life efficient, smooth and calm.

Almost 25 years later, industry analysts were only just beginning to understand the implications of Weiser's predictions as the growth of mobile devices started to seriously cannibalise personal computing. According to analyst firm Gartner, global shipments of PCs in the first quarter of 2013 dropped to under 80 million for the first time in four years. Industry commentators began to predict the rate at which personal computers would continue their inevitable decline. Again, according to Gartner in another report, by 2017 annual sales of PCs will fall to 270 million compared to 340 million in 2012. There's no let-up in the demand for computers, though – just not in the form that sits on a desk. Instead, growth is coming from personal devices, nominally thought of as telephones. The total number of computing devices, including PCs, tablets and mobile phones, is forecast to grow from just over two million in 2012 to almost three million in 2017.

Weiser didn't just suggest that computers were going to get smaller, though. He didn't just predict that they would move from desktop to handheld, from office to mobile and ultra-mobile. Weiser knew that they were set to become part of the fabric of everyday life. At the time of writing, the author is wearing a Jawbone UP wristband. This device tracks my activity levels during the day and my sleep patterns during the night. There are competitive products from Fitbit and Lark, all of which, I'm sure, are equally effective. I'm also wearing a Pebble watch, which will alert me to incoming phone calls, text messages and emails on a low-power, e-ink screen. My Pebble incorporates a magnetometer, ambient light sensors and an accelerometer. It will also tell the time.

This first generation of wearable devices are largely extensions to mobile phones, including the most high-profile wearables such as Apple Watch and Google Glass. Glass, from search giant Google, is worn like a pair of spectacles, and a prism mirror bounces light from a tiny screen into the wearer's right eye whilst allowing that eye to see through it. It works like a real-world picture-in-picture television. A front-facing camera also allows the wearer to capture pictures or video with a voice command of 'OK Glass'. One of the early adopters who signed up to the Google Glass Explorer programme was video blogger Joe Miraglitotti, who demonstrated its capabilities by recording and sharing a visit to Disneyland from his point of view, or at least the point of view of his Glass.

Connect the World

One of the most common misconceptions about wearables is that they're independent devices. Actually, wearable devices communicate with each other and with the Internet through a set of technologies that form a wireless personal area network. A smart watch isn't another piece of technology on which to make telephone calls just because the name of the incoming caller flashes on its tiny screen. This isn't a future inspired by the *Dick Tracy* watch. Instead, these devices work in concert, adding fragments of usefulness that we hadn't previously realised we needed. For example, applications such as *RunKeeper* are available on most smartphones, but checking the current pace or distance part-way through a run when the smartphone is safely encased in a neoprene armband is inconvenient. It's not *very* inconvenient. In fact, it feels a little churlish to call it inconvenient at all. Likewise, displaying some of the key information on a smart watch that can be quickly checked by a turn of the wrist is an improvement, but only a moderate one, even for the most zealous technology apologist. In aggregate, though, these tiny increases in usability usher in new possibilities. The *Tube Exits* smartphone app does only one thing: it advises London's commuters at which end of a platform they need to get on a train so that they're in the best possible position when they get off it. That's it. Only the keenest, time-impoverished, stressed-out commuters with multiple places to be on a workday morning will use it regularly. They have to find the application among the 25 or so they have on the average smartphone and enter their journey details – all ahead of entering the underground station, where they will usually lose their signal. This is one example of an app that becomes truly usable when all of those tiny barriers to use are removed and brief instructions pop up on a smart watch when you're on the platform, providing just the briefest of instruction and information at exactly the point when it's needed.

This is why wearables are only a waypoint. If we accept Weiser's predictions, computing will go way beyond wearable and personal. It will be 'in the woodwork'. Computing, Weiser argued, will be everywhere, it will be invisible, it will be ubiquitous.

Mobile and wearable computing are taking us further towards this vision of ubiquitous computing but it's less about device portability and more about computing on human terms. Today, we interact with desktop or laptop computers through apps. We share social updates in one, develop presentations in another, spreadsheets in another and check train timetables in yet another. We adapt to the app. In the near future, computing will adapt to us, it will understand our situation. *Situational computing* will sense, interpret and respond to our local and immediate environment. It will adapt to the real-world situation that we're in. In order to achieve this, computing will become increasingly fragmented – smaller grains of computing power in an increasing number of devices, all connected. Computing that was once trapped in a single device – a camera, a car, a washing machine – and isolated from the wider world is now sharing information with other apps, other devices and other services. Everyday items are becoming endowed with the ability to sense their environment, their own status, their own location, and then share this information with other objects through what has become widespread connectivity – what's referred to as the 'Internet of Things'. As this happens, our use of technology is going to change profoundly. PC users used to actively select the time, manner and duration of their interactions with the machine. In a world of ubiquitous and pervasive computing, the temperature is changed, plants are watered and journeys are diverted without much regard for the devices, data and networks that make it all happen.

Digital World

If we consider for a moment what happens when we take a journey using *Tube Exits* or when we are inspired by a *Bloom* then we get a sense of why gamification has only just become a practical possibility. These apps and many more like them assume devices that we carry wherever we go. The device must understand its own location, be connected to a high-speed network and be able to record the event with data, pictures, sound or video. It also needs an operating system common enough for developers to reach sufficient consumers to economically justify their investment in developing for the device.

The technology alone is not enough either. Digital behaviours are establishing themselves as new social norms. A billion people regularly stay in touch with their social group through a single platform, Facebook. We have largely grown tired of creating new accounts for each and every app, so open standards have emerged to enable us to set up a single personal account and enjoy many services from otherwise unrelated providers. Signing up for *Bloom*, for example, doesn't require a new account, instead users can sign up using their existing Facebook profile. This is true of many other services, too.

Mission Roundup

Analyst firm Gartner refers to something it calls 'the nexus of forces' – a set of seemingly independent technological advances that together provide new, transformational possibilities. The Gartner nexus of forces comprises social, mobile, cloud and information, all of which are independently undergoing rapid, disruptive change. Social tools are changing the way we communicate personally and professionally – and it's not just Facebook and Twitter either. Brian Solis, author of *The End of Business as Usual*, lists well over a hundred social services in Version 4 of his highly regarded infographic, 'The Conversation Prism'. Cloud services are making computing power and software convenient and affordable to the smallest of businesses and those with the most restricted personal budget. As more of what we do, say and share is digitised, we both create and have access to burgeoning data. The field of information and analytics is exploding into a new and exciting one, referred to by the wholly inadequate moniker 'Big Data'.

Seth Priebatsch, an early pioneer in gamification, believed that we would ultimately gamify the world. This requires devices, networks and software to be so widespread as to be thought of as ubiquitous. It also requires a future shaped by other innovations. Social and cloud services are part catalyst and part response to a chain reaction of new possibilities allowing for new behaviours that inspire new possibilities, and so on. Gamification is one of those new, emerging and rapidly evolving possibilities.

PART II
Motivation

Chapter 7
Intrinsicity

The Game

Consider for a moment why you're reading this book. If it's out of curiosity, because you liked the title, the precis piqued your interest or because you have an interest in organisational engagement, then your motivations are most likely from within. They're *intrinsic*. If you're flicking through the pages, feverishly scanning for the pertinent points because you have a book report to write for your manager or lecturer by the end of the week, then someone or something else is influencing you. Your motivations are *extrinsic*. The behaviour is the same – you're reading a book – but the quality of the outcomes may not be. However, when it comes to motivation, most businesses can't rely on the vagaries of human nature. Instead, they require people to behave in consistent ways so that they can deliver predictable outcomes. They need extrinsic motivators. Incentives and, hopefully to a lesser extent, punishments are essential tools to drive performance and control behaviours. However, in the rush for control, what do businesses lose? What price predictability?

The Badges

- Coin Operator

- Metric Performer

- Self-driven

- Conduct Conductor

Incentivise, Motivate, Control

In the preceding chapters, we have discussed the limitations of economic motivations in organisations. We have challenged the view that the human condition is simply one of maximising consumption whilst minimising contribution. Classic economics teaches us that our performance at work is boundlessly manipulable through incentives or punishments. Behavioural economics suggests otherwise. The most controversial fact, the most difficult to accept for many managers, is that extrinsic motivators are not as effective as we think they are. Managers in every department routinely rely on them. It's common practice to pay a portion of an employee's pay, their 'variable' or 'commission', for achieving key business metrics such as revenue or margin. A further portion may also be held back and paid on delivery against specific objectives, referred to as 'personal objectives', or 'management by objectives'. Winning a new customer, keeping discounts low, delivering a new finance system and reducing the amount of outstanding debt are all specific objectives that may result in a monthly, quarterly or annual cash bonus. Objectives like these are reviewed on a regular basis so that managers can react to changing priorities, pulling levers to deliver cash incentives in return for achieving the underlying tasks that drive business performance.

Coin Operator

There's no department that relies on incentives more than Sales. VPs or Directors of Sales will own a revenue target, the *number*, that's divided up and passed down to their teams until it lands on the desk of an individual seller as a *quota*. The sum of the individual parts exceeds the total required by the VP, so there's some room for manoeuvre. Sales quotas and commissions are as essential to Sales Departments as phones, desks, pens and paper – their presence unquestioned, their absence unthinkable. And the cost of sales incentives is not inconsiderable. In the *Harvard Business Review* article 'Motivating Salespeople: What Really Works', Thomas Steenburgh and Michael Ahearne estimate that US companies spend more than $800 billion on sales compensation – three times the amount that's spent on advertising. A sales compensation plan, or 'comp plan', is the chief motivational device for a Sales Manager. A new annual comp plan is rolled out each year, along with fanfare, flourish and, in many organisations, the promise of exotic trips for those who achieve it: sunburn for those who make the Hundred Per Cent Club, and the burning ambition that it could be them next year for those who don't.

For more than a decade, the Alexander Group has published surveys on sales compensation trends. Most recently, these have been edited by David J. Cichelli, Senior Vice President and author of *Compensating the Sales Force*. Cichelli, in an interview with Ryan Johnson of World at Work, commented that the longevity of the survey has allowed them to build an accurate picture of trends over a significant timeframe. For example, the answer to the question 'How well is our compensation plan performing?' has consistently been, in Cichelli's assessment, a third, a third, a third: a third report that their compensation plans are working well, a third that they're acceptable, and a final third that they're unacceptable. For Cichelli, a decade of analysis would suggest that compensation plans work roughly as often as they don't.

In its 2012 report *Connecting the Dots on Sales Performance*, Accenture identified that over the prior three years, 36–47 per cent of sellers didn't achieve their annual sales quotas in spite of the timing of the economic upturn. That's right – at worst, almost half of all sellers are missing their quotas. In the same report, only 10 per cent of respondents believed that their companies' compensation programmes consistently drove precise selling behaviours. As selling becomes increasingly complex, confidence in cash-for-performance compensation plans is falling.

Managing by Measuring

Various management thinkers have been attributed with the expression 'You can't manage what you can't measure,' including Peter Drucker and William Demming. Whoever popularised the expression did a great job. It can be heard echoing around offices, hallways and boardrooms around the world on any given day. If this is the case, then the Sales Team, measured on revenue, are the most manageable. All businesses measure revenue. Regardless of the part of the world they're operating in or the regulatory authority governing their business, they will be required to record and report revenues. Some, usually smaller companies, only have to report a reduced set of their financials, but it has to include revenues. Many businesses pay their Sales Teams according to the simplest form of revenue: *ordered revenue*. When a customer signs an order for goods or services, sales commissions are applied. The customer may change their mind, they may return it, the wrong product may get shipped, or there may be any number of disputes before the customer pays the invoices raised some time after the order. There are revenue recognition rules that reflect some of the complexity of matching revenues and costs within a business, but this is not reflected in orders. Relatively speaking, in any business, it's the simplest thing to measure. According to Drucker's (or Demming's) maxim, the sales team should be the easiest to manage.

The basis on which sellers can be managed and measured belies the level of sophistication with which it's applied. Sales compensation plans involve Sales Managers, Finance, Human Resources and administrators. Such is the level of sophistication that spreadsheets often fail them. When columns, rows or formulae become too complex, software solutions such as *Xactly, Workday Compensation*, SAP's *SuccessFactors Compensation* or IBM's *Cognos Incentive Compensation Management* are introduced.

Finally, Sales Departments are the most highly leveraged when it comes to financial incentives. Professional sellers can expect anything from 25 per cent to 50 per cent of their package to be tied to commissions, and sometimes more. Professional sellers don't object to the variability either. It presents an opportunity for them to earn more as a result of paying them directly for their performance. There's some bravado associated with taking a role with a greater proportion of variable pay. Indeed, it's common for sellers to feel a little derogatory about their peers in industries or roles where there's a higher basic pay and less variability. It's not 'proper' selling.

When it comes to incentives, to extrinsic motivation, there's no one more measurable, no one more sophisticated and no one group of people more committed to the customs, practices and cultures surrounding it than those who work in sales. Yet, in spite of this, the results are a third, a third, a third. The most complex, widely adopted systems of extrinsic motivational programmes fail somewhere between one in three and one in two times. Professional sellers are the most experienced, the most driven, the most accepting and the most advanced users of extrinsic motivation, yet only a third believe incentives are working well, and one in ten believe they're not driving the right behaviours anyway.

Unmotivation

The contradiction between the ubiquity and seeming unreliability of paying for performance defies conventional logic. It makes no sense to us. Paying for results should not only work, it should do so reliably. Yet there's ample evidence that cash and rewards can actually result in poorer performance. The research referred to in Chapter 4 involved four economists: two from MIT, one from Carnegie Mellon and one from the University of Chicago.

They collaborated with another institution at the centre of classical economic and capitalist thinking, the Federal Reserve System, and concluded that higher incentives lead to poorer performance. Behavioural economist, Dukes University professor and author Dan Ariely lists numerous studies in his book *The Upside of Irrationality* that demonstrate the ways extrinsic motivators erode performance. Another institution at the heart of London, of both historic and contemporary significance in global capital markets, arrived at similar conclusions. In 2009, the London School of Economics analysed 51 studies of corporate pay-for-performance plans, and concluded not just that financial incentives can be ineffective, but that they can actually reduce motivation.

Whilst managers and management thinkers attract their fair share of criticism, the practice of paying for performance rarely encounters disagreement. Almost all managers assume that if we want productivity, we need only design the right incentive programme. Alfie Kohn, in his book *Punished by Rewards*, challenges this notion. Kohn argues that rewards often impede performance on many types of tasks. He refers to Douglas McGregor, Management Professor at MIT, who developed his motivational Theory X and Theory Y back in the 1960s, as set out in his book *The Human Side of Enterprise*. Theory X suggests that people don't like work, and must therefore be coerced to take part through the offer of incentives. Theory Y, on the other hand, holds that human effort in work is as natural as it is in play. McGregor also argued that imagination, ingenuity, creativity and the desire for responsibility are widely rather than narrowly distributed across a population. Most people are smart, creative and willing. McGregor was also clear about the negative consequences of incentive plans, which included:

> *deliberate restriction of output, hidden jigs and fixtures, hidden production, fudged records ... antagonism towards those who administer the plan, cynicism with respect to management's integrity and fairness, indifference to the importance of collaboration with other parts of the organisation.* (McGregor, The Human Side of Enterprise, p. 123)

Kohn also highlights the lack of evidence to support pay-for-performance. He refers to the work of researcher G. Douglas Jenkins Jr, who collated a series of studies from the 1960s, 1970s and 1980s and found a weak or negative correlation between pay and performance. Another, and possibly the largest, review of research covered almost one hundred separate studies. The study, 'The Effects of Psychologically Based Intervention Programs on Worker Productivity', was carried out in the mid-1980s by Richard A. Guzzo, and statistical analysis indicated that there was no significant overall effect.

By contrast, training and goal-setting had a far greater impact. All the data tell us that the human desires for growth and purpose are far greater influences than purely financial incentives.

Crowding

We build motivational systems to provide clarity and direction, so that the actions of individuals align with the interests of the organisation. The assumption, though, is that they provide *additional* incentives. Most would probably complete the task or activity anyway, but the additional stimulus of a bonus increases certainty. If our organisation needs something from an individual, we reason, then adding a cash reward will make it more likely. We also assume that neither can it do any harm. Most managers would accept that not everyone is motivated by bonus payments, but they also believe that it can't cause any harm either. It transpires that this may not be the case. The reason is what Bruno Frey, author of *Not Just for the Money: An Economic Theory of Motivation*, calls 'Crowding Theory'. Frey and social psychologists such as Lepper, Greene, Deci and Ryan have variously termed this 'the undermining effect', 'the overjustification effect', 'the corruption effect' or 'the hidden cost of reward'. Intrinsic motivation, where the activity is its own reward, can be replaced by incentives – not enhanced, heightened, clarified or increased, but replaced. It's one or the other. Intrinsic motivation is diminished, replaced or crowded out by a controlling external incentive.

The Price of Failure

Achieve the result, and receive a reward; don't achieve a result, and be punished through the withholding of that reward. The result is a loss of control. Internal motivation assumes its own reward and the satisfaction of personal attainment in line with the needs of the group. Miss the goal, and the punishment is also internal, an opportunity to ameliorate. According to Nicole Lazzaro, CEO of XEODesign, gamers spend as much as 80 per cent of their time failing in video games, and it's used to learn, to improve and as an input to a strategy that will ultimately lead to success. Whilst we fail in video games most of the time, this leads to our learning, our personal pathway to improvement. Of course, the negative consequences in video games are not real, no one loses their job, there are no workplace injuries, no deal is missed, no real money is lost. However, the truth of most mistakes in business is similar.

Harvard Professor of Leadership and Management Amy Edmondson argues that the minority of what we do in the modern workplace is predictable and repeatable. Most of what we do is subject to uncertainty, and requires creativity, new ideas and novel thinking. Inevitably, this creates more opportunities for things to go wrong, and therefore more opportunities for learning. It also creates opportunities for experimenting and learning, which assumes a degree of failure. In an experiment, some things will work, some things will not. However, organisational culture rarely accepts failure as an acceptable outcome. The term 'opportunity for learning' is far too frequently euphemistic corporate language for 'This is what you did wrong.' Failure and fault are unhealthily inseparable in most companies. When Edmondson asked executives to consider how many mistakes are truly blameworthy across a whole spectrum of behaviours, they responded that it was somewhere in the region of 2–5 per cent. When asked how many are treated as blameworthy, the response was 70–90 per cent.

External rewards and punishment in the form of blame reduce the feeling of control and lessen our sense of self-determination and self-esteem. *Crowding out* is exactly this. It's not improving or enhancing motivation, as we might first think. Rather, it's replacing natural internal motivation with a synthetic one in the interest of control. There's no blame in gaming because no one really dies. In business, most mistakes are utterly retrievable, and yet few create an environment in which it's safe to fail, learn and improve.

When Crowding Out Breaks the Bank

In February 2013, HSBC announced that it was no longer paying its customer-facing staff sales commissions. Instead, they would be incentivised for customer satisfaction and quality. In an article for consumer magazine *Which?*, the head of HSBC in the UK, Antonio Simoes, was quoted as saying: 'We have changed how we assess and reward our employees, removing any sales targets, so that they can completely focus on serving our customers' needs and providing superior service.' Simoes, who holds an MBA from Columbia University, was previously a partner for McKinsey and is a contributor to the World Economic Forum, did away with sales targets to better serve HSBC's customers. Simoes removed commissions to send a message to customers that 'they can depend on HSBC to do the right thing for them'.

High street banks, institutions on which we all depend, have what might kindly be called a chequered track record when it comes to doing the right thing.

In August 2013, 13 UK high street banks and the insurer CPP were being forced to find £1.3 billion to compensate customers who were mis-sold credit card insurance policies. Many of the same banks were still paying out for mis-selling payment protection insurance at £10 billion and counting. There are other mis-selling scandals too, but all seem insignificant compared to the 2008 financial crisis, which was, at least in part, caused by high-risk borrowing, fraudulent underwriting and heavy investment in mortgage-backed securities, all fuelled by incentives that rewarded the seller for selling financial products no matter how toxic they might ultimately be to their customer. Banks pay interest to depositors and charge it to lenders, who use the money to buy houses or start or grow their businesses. They facilitate payments across international boundaries and help businesses deal with the risks associated with the fluctuating prices of raw materials and currency. When they are motivated by helping people to own their homes and businesses to manage their exposure, they are noble institutions. To do so, they need to convince us to buy their products. We don't always appreciate the complexities of currency risk, so we need to be educated and persuaded. Businesses figure that the only way to motivate one person to persuade another is to pay them a commission. When the commission crowds out the original reason why people need the products, it may end in being forced to pay back £1.3 billion.

In my role as VP of Services for Artesian, my team and I trained many hundreds of sellers in the financial services sector on *customer-centred behaviours*. These individuals are no longer called 'sellers', nor will they have the word 'sales' in their job title. Nevertheless, they offer their employer's products to their customers in return for a price in some form. What's remarkable in this new climate of regulated sales behaviours is that the most common emotion is relief. As one experienced relationship manager commented to me: 'Now we can just get on with doing the right thing. It's what we all wanted to do in the first place.'

Motivate, Create, Repeat

Corporate bonuses, commissions and incentives have their place. However, they are not the blanket solution that many organisations assume. Investing time and money in quarterly target-setting, defining objectives and incentive payments are cruder tools than we may think, and should probably be used more sparingly. They are used as corporate levers to introduce certainty, yet they can introduce unforeseen or poorly understood consequences. For example, extrinsic motivators not only crowd out intrinsic motivation, they also crowd out creativity.

Behavioural scientists divide what we do in the workplace into *algorithmic* or *heuristic*. In Daniel Pink's *Drive: The Surprising Truth about What Motivates Us*, he explains the two types of tasks. An algorithmic task is one which you follow a set of known instructions down a single path to a single conclusion. A heuristic task is the opposite. It requires experimentation, creativity and devising a novel solution. Business success in the last century was chiefly about reducing costs through scale and the efficient application of instructions, processes and policies. Even the sales process was, in the main, a script. John H. Patterson, founder of NCR, famously created a sales method that involved quota calculation, commission rates and a script that all sales staff were expected to memorise, including directions on when and where to point to the feature they were describing. In the twenty-first century, if the buying process is algorithmic, it doesn't need a seller – it can, or will eventually, be conducted online.

Research such as that conducted by Harvard Business School professor and co-author of *The Progress Principle* Teresa Amabile has found that extrinsic motivators can improve the performance of algorithmic work, but are ineffective for heuristic work. Jobs that require creativity, problem-solving and dealing with novel difficulties depend instead on intrinsic motivators. Controlling and extrinsic motivators are actually detrimental to creativity – they reduce the quality of heuristic tasks. Daniel Pink makes the same point. According to Pink's list of seven deadly flaws in his book *Drive*, extrinsic motivators can diminish performance, reduce creativity, crowd out good behaviour, encourage cheating and unethical behaviour, become addictive, and can foster short-term thinking.

Self-determination

McKinsey estimated, in their article, 'The Next Revolution is Interactions', that 30 per cent of job growth comes from algorithmic work, whilst 70 per cent comes from heuristic. Our workplaces increasingly require us to conduct heuristic work, but we are still rewarding for algorithmic work. Old systems of motivation are being used on new forms of work, and are becoming increasingly ineffective.

The volume of research to support the value of intrinsic motivation is at a level where it is, practically speaking, incontrovertible. For three decades, a global group of social scientists, including pioneers such as Edward Deci and Richard Ryan at the University of Rochester and recent scholars such as Adam Grant at Wharton School, have built a foundation of what motivates people both in and outside the workplace. Deci and Ryan were responsible for expanding earlier works on motivation into Self-Determination Theory (SDT) after Deci published a key study, 'The Effects of Externally Mediated Rewards on Intrinsic Motivation' in 1971. Since then, SDT has been validated, tested, refined and practised by a network of researchers across the world. SDT is concerned with supporting our natural tendencies, our innermost motivations, in order to promote our psychological well-being.

Like Pink and Amabile, they have found that what they call *contingent rewards* are effective for routine tasks. If you want people to screw a cap clockwise on a bottle, then the promise of a reward will excite their attention and focus them narrowly on getting the job done. Offer the same rewards for complex, creative or conceptual work, and motivation will be diminished. Offering cash incentives to create new solutions to tackle problems that are not well understood will hinder rather than help.

Autonomy Continuum

Close to 1 million of the 300 million professionals registered on the professional social networking site LinkedIn associate themselves directly to the profitability of their employer. As individuals, they own a portion of their business's total profit or loss. They indicate this in their profile as 'P&L responsibility' or 'P&L management', often adding the value they're personally responsible for: for example, 'Full P&L responsibility for a $15m budget'. Many of these individuals are effectively running businesses within businesses. Some might even use the term 'intrapreneur' to illustrate that whilst being part of a larger and established business, their attitude is entrepreneurial. It would be difficult to argue with a successful intrapreneur in receipt of a significant annual commission payment that they're being controlled by that reward, that they're being manipulated, and that any natural and personal sense of satisfaction has been crowded out. Human motivation is far more complex than this. According to Ryan and Deci in their paper 'Intrinsic and Extrinsic Motivations: Classic Definitions and New Directions', intrinsic and extrinsic exist at opposite ends of a continuum. At the far, extrinsic end is *heteronomy*, where we are controlled entirely by rewards or punishments contingent on our behaviour. At the other end is *intrinsic*, where we inherently enjoy the act itself for its own sake.

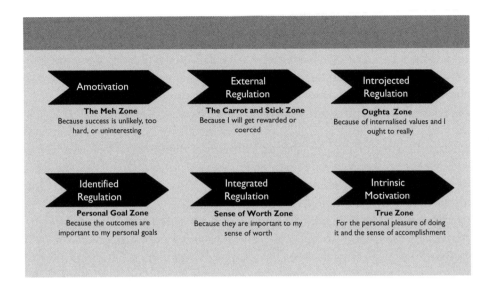

Figure 7.1   The autonomy continuum

Source: Adapted from Richard Ryan and Ed Deci, 'Intrinsic and Extrinsic Motivations'.

It's common for us to internalise external rewards. We enjoy the status they bring, are energised by the congratulations of others, and relieved at having avoided the ignominy of being excluded from the shortlist of top performers. This becomes part of us, how we identify ourselves and others identify us. We have taken on the external motivation. Ryan refers to this as 'introjection'. It has become institutionalised to a point where it looks and feels like intrinsic motivation, and is almost certainly the justification for professional sellers who willingly describe themselves as 'coin-operated'. Beyond introjection is *identification*, where the reward is external, but because we identify with it and endorse the behaviour ourselves, it doesn't entirely rely on the approval of others. Closest to intrinsic are those rewards that we have *integrated* through our social group. The social pressure is sufficient that they're almost indistinguishable from our internal motivations, even though they may not be entirely consistent with our innermost values.

In Service to Customer Service

Before businesses like Engine Yard came along, building applications required hardware, operating systems and other technical infrastructure that are not core to creating websites or mobile applications. Engine Yard provides a platform as a service that takes all of this complexity away. In doing so, it not only needs hardware, software and advanced networks, it needs a team of people to support its customers, who are typically IT professionals in finance, entertainment and governmental organisations. Many businesses have rushed to the bottom with their support teams, finding ways to reduce costs that include offshoring to lower-cost economies or outsourcing to the lowest bidder. Many, including Engine Yard, are reversing this trend in response to growing customer dissatisfaction. More than this, Engine Yard wanted to increase the level of customer engagement and encourage its support engineers to help one another. The ultimate objective is for customers to be able to find a solution quickly without the overhead of raising a new support case, whilst simultaneously freeing support engineers from routine tasks and allowing them to focus on more complex and interesting exceptions. Engine Yard used *Badgeville* to implement a simple system of recognition for contributions to the community from its internal team and their customers. A customer who searches for and finds their own solution not only saves themselves and Engine Yard time, but is rewarded with an Engine Yard Sleuth designation that progresses from Sam Spade to Lieutenant Columbo and beyond. This is straightforward gamification, but it reduced the number of support cases raised, decreased the time it took to respond, and increased engagement in forums and communities.

Engine Yard, like many support organisations, is tapping into our internal motivations to answer its own questions and those of others. It isn't doing this by paying bonuses to its employees based on call closure rates or by offering discounts to customers who self-service. Instead, it's making the contribution of others more visible through a simple system of points and badges. And whilst points and badges, in and of themselves, are extrinsic, they're also feedback loops. In digital groups like these, we are simply not going to get the positive reinforcement of someone wandering by our desk and thanking us for our help. Instead, badges and points serve less as rewards, and more as digital tokens that remind us that we have made a difference to a dispersed community.

Mission Roundup

Policy documents on developing incentive plans, and incentive plans themselves, typically mention the goals of the seller, team or organisation three times more frequently than they mention the customer. Therefore, we shouldn't be surprised that, as customers, we often feel that our objectives are not aligned with those who are supposed to serve us. Organisations have built systems of measurement and performance management that focus on the immediate needs of the business, such as revenue, profitability, response times, return on capital and employee productivity. Motivational mechanics such as bonuses for quota attainment or call handling rates are based on systems of measurement that have been designed to be predictable, measurable and repeatable, so that the business can achieve economies of scale.

Whilst external motivators achieve this, they are in fact less natural and less attuned to the way we want to work as individuals. When we introject, internalise or integrate well-designed systems of extrinsic motivations, we achieve a close approximation to aligning personal and organisational objectives. It is, however, only close. To get beyond this, we must build systems, such as those at Engine Yard, that begin to build on our personal motivations of relatedness, autonomy, mastery and purpose.

Chapter 8
Progression

The Game

There is a group of game elements that relates to our need to achieve, to progress and to improve. Of these, a running numerical count or points system is essential. Without a system to keep score and track events, there can be none of the other progression elements, such as achievements, badges, levels, medals and leaderboards. The first generation of gamified health, wellbeing, education, customer loyalty and employee engagement applications have consistently applied these devices.

However, many of these first-wave projects will fail to meet their business objectives, according to Brian Burke of Gartner in the Forbes article 'The Gamification of Business'. So if points, badges and leaderboards are fundamental game devices, are well aligned to human motivation and are being applied meticulously, why isn't it guaranteeing success?

The Badges

- Spaced Invader

- Scout's Honour

- Checking In

- The Badge Badge

High Score

Amongst the works from Roy Lichtenstein, Claude Monet and Jackson Pollock at the New York Museum of Modern Art, you will find an incongruous contribution from Tomohiro Nishikado. Nishikado is a video game designer rather than a painter or sculptor, but his cultural contribution as the creator of the video shooter game *Space Invaders* is unquestionable. It was released over 35 years ago, and had Japanese players queuing around the block as excited Asian youths patiently waited for the player in front to run out of coins. In fact, it was rumoured that so many of these coins languished in Tokyo video game cabinets that it caused a nationwide shortage of 100 yen coins, forcing the Bank of Japan to suddenly increase production.

The game was equally successful in the US when Midway, a division of Las Vegas slot machine manufacturer Bally, smelled success and licensed it for American production. Its success can be partly attributed to a renewed cultural interest in science fiction following on from the box office success of films like *Close Encounters of the Third Kind*. It would seem, however, that this was more by chance than design. Nishikado originally created the game with planes, but was unsatisfied with his attempts at animating flight. When this didn't work, he briefly considered human soldiers, but felt that this would be too violent – which seems surprising in an age when *Call of Duty* and *Grand Theft Auto* shape our sensibilities. The space theme, inspired by tentacled aliens in H.G. Wells's 1898 novel *War of the Worlds*, was a last-minute inspiration after hearing about the success of the film *Star Wars* in the USA.

Space Invaders was the first video game to introduce a high score. The few arcade games that existed in the 1970s allowed players to play until a simple end-of-game event occurred, such as a win in *Pong*. Some were even time-limited, but *Space Invaders* tracked the player's progress by assigning each alien kill a numerical value. This, along with a system of escalating difficulty and unlimited challenge, introduced the notion of progress and mastery to video games. It also introduced competition. Each machine ranked and displayed the highest scores for all to see, at least until someone unplugged the cabinet. Early gamers fought hard. Armed with a pocketful of coins, they jostled for the coveted top spot, and two important video game mechanics – points and leaderboards – were born.

Points

The first of these, points, are omnipresent in gaming. That first generation of arcade gamers received 10 points for shooting a space invader on the lowest row, 20 for one in the middle row, and 30 for one in the top row. Points are an incremental representation of progress, providing feedback to both players and games designers. They can represent a personal best, monitor who's in the lead, and ultimately calculate a winner. They are the foundation of game analytics, an in-game currency representing a common system of exchange between action and reward.

Figure 8.1   Points

Points are features of everyday life, not just in video games. They are integral to sporting activities such as football, cricket and basketball. Points systems tell us something of the historical and social conditions of the origins of the game. In tennis, for example the absence of points is noted as 'love'. Most tennis historians believe that this is because it's a mispronunciation of *l'oeuf*, the French for 'egg', but there are other theories, including the wonderful notion that in the absence of points, the player's motivation is only the love of the game. Anyone joining a group of spectators part way through a game will ask the question 'What's the score?' so that they can immediately understand the dynamics of the activity in progress. A score is chronicle, status and prediction all in a handful of numbers. Our creditworthiness is a numerical expression represented as a credit score, and we rack up loyalty points when we shop. Businesses also keep score. Their operational diversity means that there's no single system. Measurement by revenues is commonplace, but doesn't accurately represent businesses that generate long-term value through asset ownership, such as those in the financial services sector or estate management. A market demands a common scoring system, though, so public businesses are scored through their share price. Stories in the financial press about Sam Palmisano, IBM CEO until 2012, inevitably underscore his success by nodding towards the company's ever-increasing share price. IBM's own website acknowledges that under Palmisano's leadership, between 1993 and 2001, the share price increased eightfold. A corporate 'winner' can't be assessed by share price alone, though. Instead, market capitalisation – the share price multiplied by the number of shares in circulation – is probably the most straightforward method of keeping score in the real-life, global game of *Monopoly*. Apple took the lead briefly in 2012. The Cupertino consumer electronics company made the international financial headlines when its market capitalisation reached $600 billion, making it, temporarily at least, the world's most valuable company. According to the Forbes Global 2000 tenth annual ranking in 2013, Apple was back at fifteenth place in what is essentially a global corporate leaderboard using a composite score of revenues, profits, assets, share price and market value. According to Forbes, the top five companies in 2013 were Industrial and Commercial Bank of China, China Construction Bank, JPMorgan Chase, General Electric and ExxonMobil. Scoring in the global markets is a trillion-dollar business.

Gamers on the Board

Points as systems of measurement are also at the centre of managing the performance of individual businesses. Companies benchmark against their competitors by comparing market share and track their progress by scoring last years revenue against the current year. Product success is measured in sales volumes, sales execution on new business revenues, marketing effectiveness on the number of qualified leads generated, and human resource effectiveness on staff retention. Each of these appears to be simple on the surface but can be captured, calculated and interpreted in many different ways. What makes a customer 'new', a lead 'qualified' or staff turnover 'unavoidable' must be agreed, applied and understood consistently for the numbers to be meaningful and actionable. There are scores for individuals in the business, the workforce, in the form of quotas, targets and objectives. Personal measurement must align to company measurement for everyone to be successful. Like multiplayer role-playing games, successful outcomes depend on teamwork. It's social, in the sense that both the individual and the group should experience progression in harmony. Keeping count in business is not that different to game scores. Much could be taken from the way gamers continuously strive to increase their tally into improving share price, yield or gross margin. William 'Bing' Gordon, Partner at Kleiner Perkins Caufield & Byers, would have no hesitation. Gordon, former Chief Creative Officer of games producer Electronic Arts, believes that senior management teams could learn a great deal from gaming culture. Gordon told an audience in Austin,

Texas, at the annual technology event SXSW Interactive in 2012 that every Fortune 500 company should have a gamer in its executive suite. Gordon has played a significant role in the history of gaming both with Electronic Arts and as a venture capitalist investing in businesses such as Zynga. What he learned is that gamers are curious by nature. 'Gamers know if you see a door, you open it'. Not only are they inquisitive, but they also know the 'way to win is to play as fast as you can to find the edges'. Gamers very quickly intuit what works and what doesn't. Gordon passionately believes that executive teams would benefit from the experience of someone with hundreds of achievements on Xbox Live or a thousand hours on *World of Warcraft*. Those points mean they know how to work with others. In fact, *World of Warcraft*, Gordon argued in an interview for *Fast Company* magazine, is the best example of an incentive system, where strangers willingly co-operate.

Gamer points have evolved quickly from the early one-size-fits-all, running total. They don't just track the individual; they track areas of personal growth. According to Gabe Zichermann, co-author of *Gamification by Design*, there are five common types – a 'Points Palette' – which include keeping account of experience, skill, reputation and, a more recent development, karma. In addition, there are redeemable points, which serve as currency and can be exchanged for virtual goods.

Some or all of the five forms of points in Table 8.1 may feature in a gamified system. Alternatively, Zichermann points out, they may fulfil their function in the background as nothing more than a trigger for other game mechanics. This sets the scene for the next most common game element: *achievements*.

Table 8.1   Types of points

Skill	A running game score reflects mastery and progress through the game.
Experience (XP)	These track player activity. Progress and access to more difficult challenges or levels are usually dependent on higher XPs. There is typically no upper limit, and XPs can only ever increase.
Reputation (RP)	Sometimes considered a form of experience points, RPs are awarded for behaviour rather than skill. They are used in systems that require trust, and are a proxy for online, digital social reputation.
Karma	Karma points represent the Buddhist belief that whatever action you take, good or bad, eventually returns to you. In a digital world, these can be more explicitly represented. For example, users of the social reputation site Klout can award a K point to others. There's no expected *quid pro quo* – it's an exercise in karmic giving.
Redeemable	Points may be awarded for activity, but can be exchanged for virtual or physical goods. Reward programmes are an example of gamification utilising points redeemable as tangible rewards.

Source: Adapted from Gabe Zichermann and Christopher Cunningham, *Gamification by Design*.

Badges and Medals

Edward Michael 'Bear' Grylls is a writer and television presenter famous for wading rapids, climbing cliffs, ice climbing and running through forest fires. Perhaps even more notable are his dietary predilections. As the presenter of *Running Wild, The Island and Born Survivor* (*Man vs. Wild* in the USA), Grylls has been frequently dropped into inhospitable places where his survival techniques required him to eat or drink whatever's necessary, insects being amongst the least unpleasant. Grylls, at the age of 24, was the youngest Chief Scout since the role was created by Robert Baden-Powell, the founder of the Scout Movement. Baden-Powell, a lieutenant-general in the British Army, trained recruits in wilderness survival and was struck by how the soldiers he trained grew in confidence and independence. From this observation, an international programme was born that helps young people, including the young Grylls, who was a Cub Scout at age 8, to improve their confidence, leadership, teamwork and social skills. Much of their progress is observed through peer recognition using sew-on badges. Whilst Baden-Powell is well regarded, perhaps even revered, by parents, he is no doubt cursed from time to time by mums or dads who are told by their high-achieving Scout child that they need a new badge sewn onto their shirt the night before the next meeting. Had it been designed today, the system would have required that the first badge would recognise Scouts' ability to sew on their own badges. Instead, the focus is on activities including canoeing, hiking and water sports. Some do require very traditional skills, like the Pioneer Activity Badge, with rope coiling, rope sealing and anchorage. Others have a more contemporary theme, including the Global Conservation Activity Badge, focused on recycling, energy and environmental awareness.

Badges are universal symbols of human achievement. Olympic and military medals represent extraordinary, internationally recognised accomplishments. Others, such as Scout badges or those from the Professional Association of Diving Instructors (PADI) signify a personal milestone. Individual badges are often part of a system of badges. A basic PADI Open Water Diver badge is the entry level, which qualifies divers to dive alone (or at least with their buddy), and a Divemaster badge requires many more logged dives and more classroom education. There are also specialist badges for deep, cavern or ice diving, and even for swimming or diving with whale sharks.

Digital badges, medals and other tokens of achievement are perhaps the second most common video game mechanic behind points. Whilst points are continuous, badges are punctuation. Kill five opponents in *Halo 4* and you'll receive a 'Killing Spree' medal, kill 20 and you'll need to make space for a 'Rampage' medal. If an opponent kills one of your teammates and you reciprocate in kind, you may receive a few virtual slaps on the back, but you'll definitely receive an 'Avenger' badge.

Achievements, medals and badges are not just awarded for digital destruction, though. They play their part in personal growth. *Treehouse*, more correctly Treehouse Island Inc., is an online education business with a difference. Founder Ryan Carson, established a four day work week very early on to create a better balance between work and weekends for the whole company. Their progressive culture is reflected in their product too. Instead of guiding students through a structured curriculum buried in tables of text skills are represented by colourful badges. Some skills can only be attained by achieving other skills or badges first. The result is that students broaden their learning goals. They also interact with one another on shared achievements and offer advice on how others can attain the badges that are on their public profiles. There are even limited edition badges for participants in one-off workshops.

Whilst badges have continued to be de-emphasised from early gamified applications such *Foursquare* they played their part in the early rapid adoption by creating a sense of fun and curiosity. An early version of *foursquare* identified that I had mentioned my birthday in multiple check-ins, so awarded me the '16 Candles' badge. It sat alongside my 'Shutterbug' and 'Zoetrope' badges, for sharing photographs and for cinema check-ins respectively.

Badges appeal to our natural instincts to collect and to complete. The existence of a badge that marks a specific achievement can be an incentive, as can the need to complete a set of badges. It's rather like owning a trophy cabinet with a custom-shaped space for each available trophy as a regular reminder of those unattained baubles – so powerful an incentive that gamers refer to those who can't resist getting every badge or every achievement as 'completionists'. There's a degree of completionism in all of us. One of the most frequently cited examples of positive completionist behaviour is the 'Linked' progress bar. A simple, single bar representing the degree to which a LinkedIn profile has been fully written led to a significant increase in completed profiles. This was later replaced with the 'Profile Strength' meter. This is a circle in which a watermark indicates the strength. LinkedIn is an ever-changing platform, and professionals have ever-changing careers and skills, so this better reflects that some things are never complete. Progess and mastery, as motivations, are endless and infinitely rewarding pursuits.

Awards Cabinet

The value of badges isn't limited to recognition and status, but they're designed to be seen, shared and displayed. Mozilla has taken the Scout shirt out of the hut and into the networked age with its Open Badges project. It uses free software and an open technical standard to provide a platform on which any organisation can earn, manage, verify and, most importantly, display digital badges. The project is a collaboration between the MacArthur Foundation and the Humanities, Arts, Science and Technology Alliance and Collaboratory. Early adopters included the Smithsonian, Intel, NASA and the US Girl Scouts.

Taking the Lead

Leaderboards, like that list of high scores on the local *Space Invaders* cabinet, generally create a sense of competition. In their simplest form, they're a snapshot of the top few players ranked in sequence. Motivation comes from the desire to rise up the rankings – and, for some, to be at the very top.

Figure 8.2   Leaderboard

In motivating the top few with simple leaderboards, there's an obvious risk of demotivating the many. Designers of leaderboards mitigate this risk by adopting one of two approaches:

1.   **Focus on personal movements** – The focus is less on absolute ranking, and more on relative change or growth. An arrow typically indicates up, down or static relative to the previously published dashboard, along with the previous position or percentage change. The focus is more on personal improvement than competition.

2.   **Micro-leaderboards** – Players are ranked relative to a peer group. In organisations, this will typically be regional or departmental. Alternatives include groups based on experience, locality, teams or social groups.

Points Badges and Leaderboards: A Holy or Unholy Trinity?

Professor Kevin Werbach, Associate Professor at Wharton School, University of Pennsylvania, refers to points, badges and leaderboards as 'the PBL Triad' in his book *For the Win*. Werbach warns that whilst these are the most common and obvious elements of gamification, they don't, in themselves, add up to a compelling experience.

Indeed, many failed attempts at gamification are the result of the poorly considered addition of one or all of the triad. The most frequent 'failures to fly' are systems of badges. *The Huffington Post*, *Google News* and Amazon have all implemented badge mechanics, with mixed success. *The Huffington Post* was one of the first media sites to launch such a system, so it attracted a lot of attention. It would appear, though, that it has had little impact on its users' behaviours. The system is criticised for lacking context, challenge and a coherent award system. *Google News* introduced 500 in 2011, promising that the more you read their news, the quicker you would be awarded Bronze, Silver, Platinum and Ultimate badge types. In a blog post on *TechCrunch*, Robin Wauters, European Editor of *The Next Web* and Lead Editor of *Virtualization.com*, points out that reading the news is an unusual activity to reward with badges. In September 2012, Google announced that it would stop displaying badges on its online news pages as part of one of its frequent house-cleaning exercises to remove unpopular, outdated or unneeded features. Amazon also has badge systems, primarily for contributing reviews, but they also receive criticism for being uninspiring and unimaginative. Even *Foursquare*, which has pioneered the use of badges, began to de-emphasise them in its app overhaul in 2013. This, to some critics, appeared to be evidence of an outright failure of the badge mechanic, and even a failure of the entire field of gamification. Pundits appeared to delight in these failures, to such a degree that Gabe Zichermann named the phenomenon 'Badgefreude'.

Zichermann argues that badges are often maligned as ineffective but there is a danger that we will miss (pun intended) the point. Badges are an effective motivator if they are well designed, attractive, collectible and meaningful. Badges work best when they are aligned to aspirational achievements. This can be educational achievement such as that in *Treehouse* or extrinsic rewards such as the benefits awarded to frequent flyers.

They also need a structure which is either linear to a user experience or orthogonal to it. Linear badges, such as those awarded by the *Audible* audiobook app for reading, or rather listening, progressively through Newbie, Novice, Professional, Scholar and Master status. Orthogonal badges are awarded for usage or activity the player might not otherwise have taken part in. Mark up your *Audible* audiobook with notes and you are awarded the 'Stenographer' badge, listen for enough hours on the weekend and you become a 'Weekend Warrior'. These and other badges, like 'All Nighter' and 'Marathoner', are awarded for uncommon behaviours rather than for progression.

Likewise, leaderboards are amassing a chequered reputation. Poorly-designed leaderboards track the wrong metric, can be manipulated or simply don't motivate the vast majority of users because they sit squarely in the middle. Being top is, by definition, for the few and not the many, and most businesses, groups and organisations benefit from a small improvement from the entire company, not a large difference from a heroic group. The first two can easily be remedied by identifying the right metrics and the correct behaviours and leaderboards can both encourage personal and peer group improvements if designed correctly.

So the addition of one, two or all three elements of the triad doesn't guarantee successful gamification. This shouldn't surprise us. If all it took for a game to be successful was points, badges and leaderboards then all games would be successful. Clearly though, they are not. Solid design principles and thoughtful implementation are required to make game mechanics work wherever they are applied. The most common misconception though is that they only motivate us through competition and rewards. Whilst these are predictable motivators, points, badges and leaderboards are rarely just about winning, even for Bartle's Killer player type. They also tap into our need for progress and mastery and can be used as part of a design to encourage collaboration. Game mechanics that are designed to stimulate co-operation are going to be far more potent in inspiring a group and therefore in organisational gamification. According to Bing Gordon in an interview with Kevin Werbach of Wharton University 'collaboration beats competition three-to-one'. When points, badges and leaderboards are designed thoughtfully and tied to meaningful work, they appeal to our deeper needs for growth, purpose, self-determination and sociability.

Mission Roundup

Businesses measure, they count, they calculate ratios and use algorithms to predict future outcomes using a complex class of systems referred to as 'business intelligence', 'business analytics' or 'business performance management'. A subset of these systems is used to reward and motivate staff. They attempt to align organisational success with individual performance, but rarely, if ever, attempt to align to complex human motivations.

Meanwhile, video games, which only provided win–lose or time-limited conclusions during their formative years, have grown in sophistication. They were zero-sum or finite if we classify them according to James Carse, author of *Finite and Infinite Games*. It wasn't long in their evolution before a system of points was introduced that laid the foundations for levels, awards, challenges, ranking and the possibility of personal progression. Whilst it would be unrealistic to suggest that these make for endless games, they allow for prolonged and engaged play, for continuity and longevity. They represented a cultural and philosophical shift in game-play, and stimulated the human desire for progression, for personal development, for mastery.

Video games and navigating the world through digital interfaces are the new normal for anyone born after 1971. If businesses want to engage with customers and employees born after this time, then they need to see the world as they see it. They need to understand the connection between business performance management and the desire for personal progression that's being continuously satisfied over in the world of video games. They need to understand the profound levels of engagement being enjoyed as a result of games designers who have instinctively turned not just to systems thinking, but to psychology and the essence of human motivation. Progress may be just a single aspect of this, but it's a critically important one.

Chapter 9
Epic Meaning

The Game

Humanity is at war with The Covenant, an alien alliance united by their faith in an ancient civilisation known as The Forerunners and led by religious zealots known simply as The Prophets. In the distant past, The Forerunners had fought an alien parasitic civilisation, The Flood, which devoured and overran galaxy after galaxy, including our own Milky Way. The Flood were as resilient as they were insatiable, and The Forerunners, exhausted by their war with The Flood, developed a terrible weapon of unimaginable destruction as a last resort. Using an installation called The Ark, they built a series of ring-shaped megastructures that, when activated, would destroy all sentient life in the galaxy, deprive The Flood of their food, and reseed samples of all lost life forms. These giant structures were known as Halos, and gave their name to a multi-billion-dollar video game franchise. The backstory to the video game *Halo* is rich and complex, involving interplanetary systems, races, religion, colonies, political tensions, civil war and a new form of faster-than-light 'slipspace' travel. The *Halo* universe has inspired fan fiction, short stories and graphic novels. It has also been considered for as yet unconcluded film projects and live-action television adaptations.

The rich and involving *Halo* backstory set new standards for video game narrative. But what role did it play in the phenomenal success of the *Halo* franchise? Could it have been a blockbuster without it? What exactly is the significance of story in the multi-million-dollar *Halo* and the multi-billion-dollar console stories?

The Badges

- Killer App

- Story-teller

- Purposeful Play

- Purposeful Work

Epic Meaning

In Chapter 3, we referred to Jane McGonigal's defining TED Talk 'Gaming Can Make a Better World'. The talk, according to social media analytics service PostRank, now part of Google Analytics, is one of the most engaging of all TED Talks. In it, McGonigal explains that the 10,000 hours young gamers will have spent playing games by the time they reach graduation will make them extraordinarily good at four things. The first is *Urgent Optimism,* which is the desire to act immediately to tackle something they have a reasonable chance of success at completing. In business communities, this is often referred to as having a *bias for action.* Secondly, McGonigal talks about forming *Social Fabric,* or collaborating in a way that builds better relationships – in other words, we tend to like the people we play games with. The third aspect is *Blissful Productivity,* a willingness to work hard at engaging activity. And the final one is *Epic Meaning* – not just meaning, but *epic* meaning.

The dictionary definition of 'epic' is rooted in ancient story-telling traditions, describing a long poem that would chronicle the deeds and adventures of heroic figures. The *Halo* backstory follows this ancient tradition of inspiration through missions of national, global or, as it happens, interplanetary scale. Gamification commentators on the Epic Meaning meme can, however, take this a little too literally. 'Epic' can describe lofty achievements on a grand scale, but it's first and foremost a story. Byron Reeves, Professor in the Department of Communication at Stanford University and co-author of *Total Engagement,* knows more than most the impact a story can have on us. Experiments conducted by his students on the physiological impact of video games, including the measurement of heart rate and skin conductance, demonstrated that those who are offered context through narrative experience greater arousal than those who just play. The backstory makes the game more exciting. Narrative is as important to *Halo*'s game-play as the realistic graphics, the array of weaponry, points and achievements. It's no coincidence that *Halo,* the game that set new standards of narrative quality, was at the centre of one of the fiercest and most highly competitive market battles between corporate technology giants Microsoft and Sony.

Killer App

The video game market in 2013 was estimated by technology research and advisory firm Gartner to be worth close to $100 billion. There was much at stake, then, as two major players, Microsoft and Sony, battled for next-generation video game console market leadership with the Xbox One and PlayStation 4, respectively. Industry analysts at the beginning of 2014 were lining up to share their views on which machine would win, which of the two technology giants would see the best return on its eye-watering investments in engineering, manufacturing and marketing. The previous-generation console war was defined by the Xbox 360, which sold over 70 million units, the Sony PlayStation 3, which sold 80 million, and a surprising leader in the form of the family-friendly Nintendo Wii, which topped 100 million thanks to its universal appeal.

Whilst there is considerable brouhaha over the technical specifications of each console, this is only one of the variables. Ultimate success will depend upon more than graphic resolution and processing power. Microsoft and Sony will also need interesting content, available exclusively on their platforms, that is so compelling that gamers will invest in a console just so they can play that one game – the so-called *killer app*. The killer app for Xbox 360 was *Halo*. The franchise has sold more than 50 million copies, and grossed well in excess of $3 billion. The original version, launched in 2002, and its sequels set new heights in sales volumes. *Halo 3* had sales of more than $170 million on its first day, breaking the previous record held by its predecessor, *Halo 2*. The success of the franchise is in no small part a result of the strong story-telling at its centre.

Meaning

Halo was a first in this regard. Prior to *Halo*, there were examples of narrative game-play, but mostly on personal computer titles such as *Mass Effect*. In fact, the narrative director for the *Halo* series, Armando Troisi, also worked on the *Mass Effect* series at the outset of his career with Vancouver-based BioWare. In an interview at the Game Design Expo in 2013 with Garin Fahlman of the *Vancouver Weekly*, Troisi explained that narrative design is the mechanism by which stories are told. He went on to detail what he regards as the four key considerations:

1.   **narrative** – the traditional use of words and actions;

2.   **drama** – for example, digital and voice acting;

3.   **presentation** – the method of communicating the story, perhaps via a conversation or cut-scene;

4.   **interactivity** – how the story can be progressed by the player, controller in hand.

In this description, we can see that the *Halo* story involves considerably more than scene-setting or marketing. Narrative, drama, presentation and game-play touch on all aspects of the game, putting story-telling front and centre. Troisi, in another interview for the Vancouver Film School, summarised the role of narrative in game-play as providing 'a relatable context to abstract mechanics'. Troisi went on to explain that this is true of any game, not just video games. Eurogames, so called because many originate from Germany, are a form of board game that rely less on dice rolls and more on strategy. They require more thought than say *Pictionary* or *Monopoly*, but are not as serious as chess or backgammon. As much attention is paid to the story in Eurogames, such as *Settlers of Catan* or *El Grande*, as the board, rules and game pieces characteristically constructed from wood rather than plastic. The game *Small World*, for example, was devised by Belgian designer Philippe Keyaerts in 2009. In *Small World*, comical races of elves, dwarves and amazon giants battle for territories. *Small World* is generally thought of by the Eurogamer community as a re-implementation of *Vinci*. *Vinci* was also devised by Keyaerts, and has almost identical mechanics and rules. The narrative theme, though, is different, focusing instead on European geography and ancient civilisations. This fundamentally changed the way in which what was effectively the same game was received. Today, it's difficult even to find an English-language copy of *Vinci*, whilst the colourful and humorous narrative underpinning *Small World* continues to make it a commercial success for publishers Days of Wonder.

Narrative alters our perception. It changes the way we understand the abstract, but it also changes the way we understand nuanced or complex situations. Companies are often multi-faceted, with multiple stakeholders, a wealth of products, customers who operate in different markets, and a variety of channels to reach them. Stories reduce global industries, processes and matrixed organisation charts to a human scale. An example of the good things a customer has achieved is far more powerful than a mission statement or carefully crafted marketing copy. In narrative, we find context, and context is how we relate to the work we do each and every day.

Narrative, Purpose and Engagement

John Marshall and Matthew Adamic's article 'The Story is the Message: Shaping Corporate Culture' in the *Journal of Business Strategy* concludes that narrative is a key element in defining corporate culture, and is far more powerful than dress code, working hours or anything else that might appear in the employee handbook. In a series of interviews with organisational leaders noted for their corporate story-telling, the article concludes that stories inspire, motivate and have emotional appeal that is absent from facts, figures and institutional reports. We all, according to the article, want our work lives to be part of a grander and more important story. Former CEO of Boeing Phil Condit is one of those interviewed who has experienced the power of corporate story-telling time after time. Condit identifies Southwest Airlines and his counterpart at the time, Herb Kelleher, as exemplars. The Southwest Airlines story is a refreshing alternative to the usual anodyne corporate vision statement. Southwest Airlines sought to 'democratize the skies'. Its narrative is an irreverent one. Kelleher once armwrestled the CEO of a competitive airline for the right to use the slogan 'Just Plane Smart', and both companies donated a proportion of the money that would have gone to legal fees to charity. When Northwest Airlines ran an advertisement claiming to be the number one airline, Southwest ran an ad that read 'Liar, liar. Pants on fire.'

This narrative is not just folklore and rhetoric either. It earns enviable engagement. According to social employee site Glassdoor, which allows employees to rate benefits, career opportunities, management, culture and values, Southwest employees love their company. Almost 90 per cent would recommend the company to their friends. More employees would recommend Southwest in this way than Virgin Atlantic, British Airways, American and United. What's more surprising, given the typically unsociable industry shift patterns, is the fact that the percentage who would recommend Southwest is higher than Apple, and almost as high as Google. Southwest's narrative and purpose drives senior executives in their decision-making too, providing 'landing lights' for difficult commercial situations. Roy Spence Jr, author of *It's Not What You Sell, It's What You Stand For*, who worked closely with Kelleher, describes Southwest's purpose as its 'North Star'. Spence, in the article 'How P&G, Southwest and Google Learned to Sell With Noble Purpose' by Lisa Earle Mcleod for *Fast Company*, described a situation where, during difficult times for the airline industry, consultants recommended that Southwest should start charging for bags. The consultancy firm had done its maths too. Not only were all the other airlines doing it, but it would immediately add $350 million to the bottom line. The leadership team said no. They didn't pull together a spreadsheet, and they didn't run it by their accountants before doing so either. They didn't need to. It ran counter to their narrative, it violated their purpose. Charging for bags wouldn't give more people the chance to fly, it wouldn't make the skies more democratic. Instead, they reminded their customers of the Southwest story. They launched a 'Bags Fly Free' campaign, and nine months later the consultants were forced to admit they had made a mistake. By publicly sticking to its purpose Southwest, drove an extra $1 billion in new revenue and took market share from its competitors.

We Were Thirsty

Yale School of Management Professor Barry Nalebuff discovered that he shared a passion with his student Seth Goldman during a class discussion of a Coca-Cola versus Pepsi case study. Both men were frustrated that whilst global beverage corporations had the might to distribute drinks around the planet, they failed to provide anything other than health risks and sugary-sweet or tasteless beverages. In 1998, the two founded Honest Tea to provide organic drinks, ethically sourced, and either unsweetened or naturally sweet. The mission statement on Honest Tea's website is a long way away from the usual insipid corporate prose. It quickly becomes narrative, the organisation's story. The story was so important to the company that Nalebuff and Goldman wrote a book, *Mission in a Bottle*. As you would expect, the book is open, honest and full of humility. What's less expected, perhaps, is its graphic novel format. In 2011, the Coca-Cola company purchased Honest Tea. This might seem a curious move, given that Nalebuff and Goldman were motivated by the notion that every bottle of Honest Tea consumed was one less sugar-loaded equivalent consumed by another human being. It would be tempting to think that Nalebuff and Goldman sold out their original story to the very company that they disrupted. However, this is far from true. In an interview for *The New York Times*, Goldman explained that the acquisition meant they could expand the availability of their brand. Their aspiration now was to be the first mainstream organic beverage. The acquisition was no sell-out. When Coca-Cola executives asked Honest Tea to remove the words 'no high fructose corn syrup' from the packaging because it was an implied criticism of Coca-Cola's products, Goldman refused, and Coca-Cola accepted the decision. They all knew that the decision demonstrated that Honest Tea stood for something. Coca-Cola bought in, Goldman and Nalebuff didn't sell out. It's easy for an employee to feel engaged with the Honest Tea narrative. Like Southwest, engagement can be seen 'in between the lines' of reviews from its own employees on Glassdoor, too. The reviews are candid. Comments about the hard work and long hours often required in a fast-growing, early-stage company ring true with my own experience in such businesses. However, they also paint a picture of people who genuinely care about their products, are invested in the culture and feel valued.

Noble Purpose

Narrative purpose is not the prerogative of agile, entrepreneurial businesses intent on disrupting established markets. Nor is it the prerogative of charismatic, armwrestling leaders. In her book *Selling with Noble Purpose: How to Drive Revenue and Do Work that Makes You Proud*, Lisa Earle McLeod carefully composes a list of companies that whilst they might appear ordinary, have carefully crafted a narrative that describes their noble purpose. This includes Virginia based Graham-White, a company that's almost a hundred years old and manufactures heavy-duty valves, compressors and other components for the transportation industry. It might be tough to find narrative and purpose in a company that makes compressors, but their sales team do so. Ask a Graham-White seller what they do, and rather than tell you that they're 'a transportation component sales rep', they'll explain that if you're on a train and moisture gets into the air system, cold temperatures may cause the moisture to freeze and the brakes won't function properly. They stop this happening. Their purpose is to make transport safer, faster and more reliable. The stories don't stop at their purpose either. Locomotive engines are always in service, which makes it challenging to service items like the brakes. One Graham-White representative didn't want to miss the moment a locomotive came back into the shop yard even though it was getting late at night. Returning to his hotel room would have meant losing at least 30 minutes, so he decided to sleep in his car. And it was snowing. When the customer called him at 3 a.m. and he showed up at his desk little more than a couple of minutes later, he cemented his status as a legend. When one of the older reps shared the story at a session facilitated by McLeod, she couldn't help but notice that everyone in the room stood just a little taller. That's the power of a human story.

Me.2.0

According to Mihály Csíkszentmihályi, author of *Flow: The Psychology of Optimal Experience*, we don't buy products. Beyond the basics, such as food and security, we buy to create a better version of ourselves. Clothing, cosmetics and even soft drink marketers have been tapping into this for decades. We buy for a purpose, and that purpose is never, ever shareholder value.

Most understand that it's a natural outworking of successful business, but few are inspired to buy from or work for a company as a result of its being part of, let alone the core of, its story. Companies need capital to start up, innovate and grow, and the capital they use must generate a return for those who provide it. However, it generates little emotional engagement in us. We don't buy from or invest our time or work in vendors to make them money. It's an outcome, not a purpose. In fact, when shareholder value becomes the primary purpose, we don't just disengage, sometimes we punish companies. In 2013, UK customers rounded on Starbucks because the company hadn't paid domestic Corporation Tax. Regardless of the facts, the complex accounting practices of multinational corporations were simply less powerful than the unfolding story, which resulted in Starbucks committing £20 million over two years. In an article for *The New York Times* in February 2012, former Goldman Sachs Executive Director Greg Smith announced that he was resigning after twelve years at Goldman Sachs because the 'interests of the client continue to be sidelined in the way that the firm operates and thinks about making money'. Smith wrote: 'not one single minute is spent asking questions about how we help clients. It's purely about how we can make the most possible money.' The article was the most emailed article over the next few days, and Goldman Sachs saw $2.15 billion wiped off of its market value. This is what happens when we, as customers, discover that the story doesn't have us at the centre and that our roles are merely as pawns or puppets for profit. Enduring companies have stories that their customers can relate to. The late Steve Jobs wanted to build a company to make great products, Southwest democratises the skies by keeping fares low and spirits high. Honest Tea believes that every bottle it sells means one less bottle of a drink containing high fructose corn syrup that someone will drink. Packaging company Tetra's story is not about boxes. No, its narrative is to 'make food safe and available everywhere'. Narrative purpose is not soft, fluffy nostalgia and fairytale either. It makes good sense, and it makes good business sense if those things should ever be separated. Purpose impacts share price. Motley Fool equity analyst Todd Wenning wrote in a 2009 article on its website that 'The greatest stocks of the next generation will be companies with a tremendous sense of purpose led by passionate executives who are guided by that purpose and not solely by profits.' Epic Meaning can move the share price.

Mission Roundup

The gamification community don't all agree that Epic Meaning is a bona fide game mechanic. Whilst it's widely referenced by practitioners some, such as Tadhg Kelly and Andrzej Marczewski, argue that it relates more to motivation or outcomes. In its most literal sense, though, it's both. Meaning, a sense of purpose, is a fundamental human motivation. Epic is the ancient art of story-telling, the means by which meaning is ascribed, the mechanic.

Story-telling pre-dates writing. The earliest cave dwellers daubed symbols on their walls as a way of remembering stories. Most of us still have symbols of stories displayed in our homes in the form of DVD jewelcases, movie posters and book covers. It's no accident that, even on digital equivalents, those symbols remain. Apple's *Cover Flow*, an animated three-dimensional graphical user interface that simulates flipping through album covers and movie artwork, feels so natural because of these same symbols. Paul Smith, former Consumer Research Executive of Procter & Gamble and author of *Lead With a Story*, has spent more than twenty years observing what it takes to motivate, inspire and persuade others. His conclusion is that it's story-telling. From the CEO addressing the board of directors to the conversation around the coffee machine, human narrative has the power to engage and inspire. Organisations that can build and live a meaningful and authentic narrative are giving their employees something they can truly engage with – *purpose*.

Chapter 10
The Sandbox

The Game

Role-playing games (RPGs) have their roots in the 1970s phenomenon *Dungeons and Dragons*. The game was played with pencil, paper and a complex series of tables, statistics and multi-sided dice. For many, it conjures up images of awkward teenage boys pretending to be knights, heroes or elves as an alternative to 'healthy' social interaction. Indeed, some churches during the 1990s suggested that playing *Dungeons and Dragons* was an 'entry point' – a start on the slippery slope of satanic worship. Neither view withstands scrutiny. Instead, set in fantasy worlds, *Dungeons and Dragons* is an interactive form of story-telling, with each player taking their part in the narrative directed by a dungeon master, who had to be part-author and part-referee. It requires a vivid imagination and that participants interact and collaborate around a story utilising social skills as advanced as any other group activity. Its primary demographic, settings and complexity nevertheless made its journey from tabletop to computer screen inevitable.

Role-playing games, as the name suggests, start with the freedom to create a personality, a role, a character. Players may rely on brute strength as a dwarf, cunning, stealth and guile as thief, or magical prowess as a wizard. Decisions made in an RPG might even impact the personality of the player within the game. Both BioWare's *Star Wars: Knights of the Old Republic* and Lionhead Studios' *Fable* series use advanced systems of ethical and moral development. The player's character is a blank slate, a block of marble waiting to be chiselled and shaped by player choice. Behaviour even shapes the characters' appearance in these games. Immoral behaviour not only harms the reputation of the characters, but they also develop dark and shadowy features. Accusations of generalising and stereotyping aside, RPGs introduced choice at a fundamental level in gaming. Other types of games, however, introduced even more alternatives, some almost limitless in possibility, merely providing a destination, with very few rules on how the player might arrive there. New genres emerged, such as sandbox, open-world and turn-based strategy.

The impact on computer and video gaming was remarkable. It opened up entirely new audiences previously uninterested in what the console or controller had to offer. Why was this? What was it about these new forms of video games that took us beyond space travel, platform jumping and explosions that had an appeal that was entirely across-the-board?

The Badges

- Sim Sim

- Turn by Turn

- I Did It My Way

- In It for the Duration

Doll House

In 1984, video game developer Will Wright was working on the game *Raid on Bungeling Bay*. The game required the player to pilot a helicopter over enemy territories, destroying weapons factories. On the surface, it was an action-oriented game much like many others. Underneath, though, the game tracked resources through an industrial food chain, allowing players to approach the game in more strategic way. As an action title, *Raid on Bungeling Bay* was well received, but Wright had been more interested in the strategy, the coastlines, the roads and the bridges than the raiding. After the game had been completed, he continued to invest his creative energies in the mapping, and added the ability to create roads and buildings. He also added real-world elements, such as population growth, taxes, crime rates and zoning, and a new game, *Micropolis*, emerged. Wright touted his invention around video game companies, but their reaction was unenthusiastic at best. It was unlike any other title at the time. There was no collecting coins, no straddling platforms and no princess to rescue. Where was the fun, they figured, in laying water pipes, designing road layouts and urban zoning? Who would want to be a city planner in their free time? It looked like it would be confined to obscurity, until a chance meeting with an up-and-coming software publisher, Jeff Braun, at the home of a mutual friend in 1987. They eventually formed their own company, Maxis, and after a few tweaks, including a name change, *SimCity* was released. Its open-ended nature and realistic themes – the original reasons for its negative reception with the established industry – set it apart. It appeared in articles in *Time* magazine and the *New York Times*, for the first time attracting an adult audience to gaming. With the release of *SimCity*, an entirely new genre was born.

The original game and the inevitable sequels sold in their millions, and have been some of the best-selling games of all time. Maxis didn't limit the franchise to cities either. It applied the 'Sim' prefix to just about everything that could be simulated – including islands, parks, planets and ants. However, not all titles were as successful as Wright's urban planning simulation, and their business was ultimately acquired by video game giant Electronic Arts (EA) in 1997. The 'Sim' idea had not yet run its course for Wright, and shortly after the acquisition, he and a single seconded programmer presented an idea they called *Dollhouse* to EA. Wright had tested the idea before with the Maxis board, and the new owners regarded it in the same way – cautiously. Wright had been right many times before, but the concept sounded like it would be completely unappealing to young males, still their primary audience. EA reluctantly went along with Wright, and in February 2000, the first life-simulator, *The Sims*, was released. The degree to which it was successful surprised everyone, including Wright. He had hoped to sell a million copies. A million copies, he figured, would vindicate the idea. It ultimately sold 16 million copies, overtaking the then best-selling PC game *Myst*. The sequels and expansion packs sold tens of millions of copies, and at over 150 million copies, it became the best-selling PC franchise in history. Its impact on popular culture, though, is even wider-reaching. In order to create a game that appealed globally, *The Sims* uses a fictional language called Simlish – a fusion of real languages, including English, French and Latin. Even the songs in *The Sims* are sung in Simlish, including the hugely popular 'Mayzie Grobe'. Katy Perry, Depeche Mode, Nellie Furtado and Lily Allen have all recorded versions of their own songs in Simlish. The Black Eyed Peas not only recorded versions of 'Shut Up' and 'Let's Get It Started', they also wrote and recorded songs for *The Sims* games.

Wright and Maxis changed video gaming for ever. Before *SimCity*, this field of entertainment was constrained to a narrow set of themes, and an even narrower demographic. The *Sims* franchise set the scene for *Second Life*, *FarmVille*, *World of Warcraft* and an entire genre of video games that allowed players to explore and design. They took gaming into diverse domains such as architecture, astrophysics and urban planning. They changed the way women thought of video games, too. More than 20 per cent of *SimCity* players were female – four times as many as the average game before it. *The Sims* broke away completely, appealing mostly to females. Most importantly, though, Maxis games were not limited by win/lose outcomes. They were the very definition of infinite games, according to James Carse's *Finite and Infinite Games*. Finite games are played for the purpose of winning. To Wright, however, there's nothing more important than the joy of the game itself. *SimCity*, for example, doesn't tell you how to win. Instead, the player decides whether the goal is to build a city that makes money, has low crime, low pollution or works entirely around public transport. Games like *SimCity* and *The Sims* are not engaging because they're escapism – they're not. They don't engage us through the spectacle. Setting taxes, parking fine levels and scrubbing virtual kitchens couldn't be more ordinary, even mundane. Instead, they open up a rich network of choices, clear rules and opportunities to build a city, an economy or a life, all within your own complete and utter control. Their appeal is rooted in our desire for autonomy.

Choice by Turn

If there's one name as high-profile as Will Wright in the field of inventive gaming, it's Sid Meier. A survey of 9,000 game developers commissioned by the Develop Conference placed Meier fifth in a list of development heroes. Shigeru Miyamoto, creator of *Mario*, *Donkey Kong* and *The Legend of Zelda*, took first place. Meier, then, is in a list of five that includes Miyamoto; John Carmack, the lead programmer for *Doom*; David Jones, the creator of *Grand Theft Auto*, and Will Wright.

When video game production values started to require Hollywood-sized budgets, Meier designed a visually uninspiring two-dimensional game that involved little more than a series of interesting decisions. The turn-based strategy game *Civilization* endured two decades, four sequels and any number of accolades, including *Computer and Gaming World*'s number one best game of all time. What it lacked in graphical sophistication, it made up in ambitious scope. The player chose a nation during 4000 BC, and year by year, turn by turn, developed a single settlement into cities, technologies, wonders of the world and, of course, armies. Some games are addictive, but *Civilization*'s blend of exploration, economics, research and conflict made it frighteningly so. I, for one, have said to myself 'Just one more turn' as the birds have started singing outside my window.

Turn-based strategy games, like simulation games, provide a wide range of choices. The key difference, however, is that there's a set of victory conditions. *Civilization*, for example, allowed economic, diplomatic and technological victories. The player often takes on the mantle of leader or ruler in a turn-based game.

The sense of control and potency amidst an almost limitless set of options is so great that games such as these are sometimes referred to as 'God Games'.

The nonlinear design of simulations and turn-based titles expanded the appeal of video games. Their free-roaming nature tapped into motivations that earlier video games had missed. The most open of open-world games is described as a *sandbox*, the epitome being *Minecraft*, in which players live in a world comprising low-resolution cubes which they can combine and process as materials. The materials can be used to build anything. Players make the most of their freedom, building ships, landscapes, buildings and even a full-scale model of *Star Trek*'s USS *Enterprise*, complete with turbolift and an external access port. *Minecraft* wasn't created by a large development studio and published by a major name. However, the lack of marketing coverage or huge development budgets hasn't prevented independent developers Markus 'Notch' Persson and Jens 'Jeb' Bergensten selling more than 30 million copies. *Minecraft* is a rare thing – a video game recommended by teachers. It's widely used in education. Geography teachers encourage children to build real-life villages, whilst physics teachers use it to illustrate fluid dynamics and mechanical properties. The game engenders creative passion, and I wouldn't be surprised if, in 30 years' time, I'm introduced to an architect, physicist, engineer or programmer who tells me that the source of their professional inspiration was *Minecraft*.

Purpose Without Method over Method Without Purpose

Games such as *SimCity, Civilization* and *Minecraft* defy conventional views of video gaming. They're not violent, they're played up and down generations and across genders, and they require deep reflection more than rapid reflexes. Their almost universal appeal can be attributed to the degree to which they satisfy our innate human need for autonomy. They provide purpose without prescribing the method by which it can be achieved. There's a broad definition of success, but players determine their own path towards it.

Compare this with how work can be typically designed for the industrial age. Outcomes are achieved through a series of tasks, each designed for minimum variation. The outcome needn't necessarily be understood, only its part in the process. The purpose of a flight attendant is to ensure that passengers are safe and satisfied throughout their flight. The job specification of a flight attendant, however, will quickly gloss over the purpose and settle down into pages of duties, activities, processes and responsibilities. Of course, these will all be entirely sensible, and even embody best practices from a wealth of airline experience. Given that they represent airline safety, they will be extremely well thought through and carefully considered. Nevertheless, each additional step increases the risk that it may conflict with another in certain, perhaps unforeseen, circumstances. More importantly, as each policy item is documented, there's a corresponding reduction in the autonomy of the individual who will carry it out. Whilst there's an obvious need for instruction and guidance, it's rarely balanced with individual freedoms, innovation and creativity. Policies and procedures quickly become legalistic, constraining natural creativity and all but eliminating autonomy.

On a recent visit to Hawaii, I returned my hire car on day two because I was concerned that it was unsuitable for some of the track roads from which we planned to hike. I had prepaid for fuel on the original car, but had barely used an eighth of the tank before returning it. The car hire staff were clearly very experienced and had been with the company and on the island for many years. However, they couldn't find a way to charge me for the eighth of a tank used in the returned car in order that I could 'carry over' my prepaid fuel plan to the new car. There was much debate about which set of keystrokes on their system would achieve the outcome everyone wanted, but after interminable experiments with the keyboard, I conceded my prepaid fuel status on the new car, offering to return the tank full just so that the staff could get on with serving other customers and I could get back to my holiday. The processes were all carefully designed and supported by sophisticated systems, yet one traveller replacing a larger car with a smaller one broke them. The situation wasn't particularly complex, nor, dare I say, particularly unpredictable. The staff were clearly smart and well trained, and their customer wasn't putting them under any time pressures. Nevertheless, their ability to deal with this relatively simple exception was clearly hampered and hindered by systems and process, rather than helped. I didn't leave unhappy, but then I was in good spirits and a holiday mood. Nevertheless, all of us, staff and customer, concluded our interactions with a vague sense of frustration and feeling not entirely satisfied. We all *knew* what the right thing to do was, but were constrained by the processes and systems such that the staff couldn't act autonomously.

In a post on Jeff Kober, author of *The Wonderful World of Customer Service at Disney*, describes the problem with trying to build processes that deliver the legendary Disney customer service levels:

> *The typical tendency for leaders is to try and map out all of the possible behaviors their employees should demonstrate when working with customers. This approach is flawed for two important reasons.*

First, such behaviors tend to come across as rote, rather than genuine. Second, it is impossible to map out all the potential behaviors individuals should demonstrate for future unforeseen circumstances. (Jeff Kober, 'Disney Service Basics', n.p.)

Kober was rejecting the process world wholesale because it didn't deliver what customers, or guests, had come to expect from one of the world's best-loved brands – open, genuine, reciprocal and human exchange that can't be mapped in a process, but comes from an engaged employee, enabled and empowered to do the right thing. Autonomy and autonomy-focused games seem to be the opposite of overly bureaucratic systems and processes. The former epitomise purpose without method, the latter method without purpose.

Need for Speed

Like mastery and progression, we have a need for autonomy – not a desire, but a need. Richard Ryan, Professor of Psychology, Psychiatry and Education at the University of Rochester, speaking at a symposium in Bath in the UK in 2012, explained what we mean by 'needing' autonomy. It isn't 'need' in the same way that I needed an iPad Air, a Jawbone UP or any of the other items of technology that impatiently sit on my Amazon or Apple wishlists. A need is something essential to our physical and psychological well-being. We need food and water, we don't need retina screens or wearable technology. This applies to what we say we don't need, too. Some may say that they don't need vitamin C, but they do. There's objective evidence that the absence of certain vitamins in our diet will have a negative physiological effect. Some might also say they don't need companionship, that they're natural loners, happier in their own company. However, there's overwhelming evidence to suggest that we need to feel connected to others, and that it increases our sense of well-being. Relatedness, connecting with others, objectively has a positive psychological effect.

Thanks to Ryan and his long-time collaborator in this field, Ed Deci, Gowen Professor in the Social Sciences at the University of Rochester, we know that we need autonomy. Their research has been exhaustive. When we feel autonomous, we're happier and healthier. We also work harder and more effectively.

Autonomy Over Compliance

The sheer volume of research conducted by Deci and Ryan on the subject of autonomy has resulted in their establishing an important and influential theory on human motivation: Self-Determination Theory. According to hundreds of studies carried out by Deci and Ryan, we manifestly need autonomy. Daniel Pink, author of *Drive: The Surprising Truth about What Motivates Us*, describes what autonomy means to the workplace. 'Control', according to Pink, 'leads to compliance', whilst 'autonomy leads to engagement'. Compliance will keep people at their desks, tills, counters, machines and stations during the day, but if we want a team to go through the night for an important deadline, we need engagement. However, out of all the workplace human motivations, it's the most misunderstood. We tend to assume that it's a solitary state of mind, individualistic, working without restraint and without collaborating or co-operating with others. Deci and Ryan would disagree.

What It is to be Autonomous

Autonomy, for example, is not unconstrained choice, it is not complete freedom. In fact, unconstrained choice can erode our sense of purpose, it can dilute our sense of autonomy, and it can lead to us drifting. As a younger man, with more free time, I picked up one of the earliest sandbox games, *Elite*. *Elite* allowed you to pilot a somewhat cranky old ship around a seemingly infinite universe, picking up paid missions which allowed you to upgrade your craft and take on more difficult and well-paid missions. I spent hours diligently adding more cargo space, better weapons and faster engines. It was an immersive experience in spite of its very basic line-drawn graphics. Then one day I found a hack. A series of button presses gave me unlimited credits. I was able to purchase every upgrade, reach any point in the Galaxy and take on any mission. I had complete freedom. After that evening, I never played it again. Stripped of purpose, the game no longer satisfied my need for autonomy.

Nor does autonomy mean 'independent', even though the fact that many games can be played solo suggests this. We can be dependent upon a doctor when we're feeling unwell, a language teacher when we're learning a new tongue or a lawyer when drawing up contracts, but this doesn't imply that we're not autonomous. We're dependent, but we're acting autonomously. Deci and Ryan would refer to this as 'volitionally dependent'.

Most importantly for organisational autonomy, it doesn't mean that we only act on our own initiative. It's not the complete absence of external direction. Assuming we have a belief in social order, we're likely to follow the instructions of a police traffic officer diverting us away from our usual route home. Taking guidance from a coach or direction from a manager doesn't deny us autonomy. We can still be acting volitionally.

So, whilst we intuitively think of autonomy as acting in isolation, independently or without influence, it's not really any of these things. Instead, according to philosophers including Paul Ricoeur, Alexander Pfänder and more recently Marilyn Friedman, Chair of Philosophy at Vanderbilt University, Tennessee and feminist writer, it can be summarised as 'acting in a manner consistent with our inner self and our own values'. Whilst it's not the absence of influence, autonomy can't be imposed upon us. In fact, the opposite of autonomy, heteronomy, is acting as a result of force outside of oneself. It's subordination or subjection. Autonomy is about congruence, and living a life that reflects your deepest values, wants and needs. It's self-determination.

Acting autonomously not only makes us happier and healthier. When we act autonomously, we're more successful. Numerous studies, including those from Deci and Ryan, have found that students who are involved in setting their own educational goals are more likely to reach them. When students perceive that the primary focus is to obtain external rewards, they perform more poorly, regard themselves as less competent and report greater anxiety. Students who are motivated by rewards for good grades or guilt trips for poor ones just don't perform as well. What's more, studies conducted in rural areas and wealthy suburban areas yielded the same result, as did studies of American, Japanese and Chinese elementary school children. Self-determined students performed better. There are many other studies that support the success of self-determination. One, a study of long-term weight loss in Portuguese women, in the journal *Medicine & Science in Sports & Exercise*, predicted that those who were self-determined from the outset were still exercising regularly twelve months later. These and other studies suggest that autonomy isn't culturally specific, it isn't influenced by geography, urban density, gender or age. Universally, the more autonomy is evident, the more positive behaviours persist.

Mission Roundup

Interestingly, long-term engagement is also evident in autonomy-focused games. In their book *Glued to Games*, Scott Rigby and Richard Ryan identify that autonomy is the most significant contributor to the desire to re-engage with a game over the long term. Games that satisfy a sense of mastery and achievement are, like a Hollywood blockbuster action movie, fun at the time. However, a rich sense of autonomy is the strongest indicator that a game session will be longer and that there will be a sustained motivation to play the game over many months, even years. Our sustained engagement, it would seem, is earned through providing a strong sense of autonomy.

The games that shifted the way we think about video games and opened them up to entirely new players didn't have next-generation graphics, explosive visual effects, Hollywood tie-ins or orchestral scores. Instead, they tapped into something essential and universal about the human experience: *autonomy*. It would also seem that this same quality keeps players at their console or keyboard longer. They engage their players more deeply and for longer than any other type of game.

Whilst some texts on the subject of gamification focus on choice, the success of this genre of gaming hints at something more fundamental. Autonomy is more than the option to be a wizard or a warrior, deeper than representing and customising your virtual self as an avatar. It's more than choice. Autonomy is the freedom to make choices that are consistent with your beliefs, with your deepest sense of self, and the connection between this and our engagement is as evident as it is undeniable.

Chapter 11
Massively Multiplayer Work

The Game

Although Sam and Dan Houser were sons of Walter Houser, co-owner of Ronnie Scott's famous London jazz club, their musical preferences lay elsewhere. Their love of American East Coast rap and hip-hop eventually led them to work at BMG records, where they scouted for and signed British acts before eventually moving to BMG Interactive, the video game division. Here, the brothers intended to attract edgy rap culture titles, but early releases neither reflected their cool brand aspirations nor performed well. This all changed when David Jones from Scottish developers DMA pitched a PC title called *Race'n'Chase*.

The player could take on the role of a policeman, or that of a petty thug with aspirations for the criminal big time. The criminal missions involved assaults and contract murders, with practically free rein in a virtual metropolis, Liberty City, where almost any car could be stolen. Dan would later recall that the game would run for only a few seconds then crash, but for the brief time he was able to play the game, he 'understood the magic'. It was dark, anarchic and edgy. It was different to anything they had seen before. The Houser brothers had discovered their first rapper-inspired title. The game evolved. Players could only be gangsters, achieving progress through delivering drugs, mugging citizens and committing violent crimes, including vehicular manslaughter. They renamed it *Grand Theft Auto* (*GTA*), and released it in 1997, exciting a wave of controversy.

GTA is a multi-billion-dollar franchise. It's the game that characterises every parental fear about video gaming. It's a tough ask for even the most liberal to see the positive in a game which seemingly celebrates casual violence. At its best it's a time-wasting, immersive sandbox city in which careers, relationships and exam results are sacrificed at an altar of flaming Ford Mustangs. At its worst, critics allege, it's behind dissociative behaviour, copycat urban rampage and violence wrought upon society by an increasingly isolated and desensitised youth. Most new communication media have been ushered in with concerns about their impact on our mental and physical well-being, and this is never more true than those that are adopted by the world's youth. Does the interactive nature of video gaming make it different, though? Will this new, rapidly evolving medium be a force for social decay, or will history repeat itself and present new opportunities for social cohesion?

The Badges

- Super Better

- Super Happy

- Super Social

Anti-social

The Pan European Game Information (PEGI) system rated *Grand Theft Auto V* as suitable for players aged 18 and over. The US equivalent, the Entertainment Software Rating Board (ESRB) similarly rated it 'Mature'. Such bodies do their best to be objective about the *Grand Theft Auto* franchise. Others, though, have taken a more emotional view. New York City officials spoke out about its inaccurate depiction of crime levels in the city supposed to have inspired the game. It also decried a system of point scoring that relied on injuring and killing police officers. Politicians, victim support groups, nonprofits and many other organisations added their voices to the outcry. Some nations threatened bans, and others, including Australia and New Zealand, vowed to release only edited versions of the game. Few ever did so, as a result of public pressure and petitions.

In 2008, a group of teenagers were arrested in New York after a crime spree that was, according to reporters, inspired by *Grand Theft Auto*. The group, armed with baseball bats, crowbars and broomstick handles, attacked and mugged a man in New Hyde Park and smashed a passing van. This was not, by any means, the only violent crime linked to *Grand Theft Auto*. That same year, Reuters reported that a teenager who robbed and murdered a taxi driver had done so in imitation of the game. Much later, in August 2013, Sky News reported that an eight-year-old boy grabbed a gun and shot his grandmother just minutes after playing one of the many sequels to the original version, *Grand Theft Auto IV*.

Whilst *Grand Theft Auto* has become the most widely known example of controversial video games, the list of games that have caused public outrage is long. It includes titles such as *Saints Row* from Volition and *Mortal Kombat* from Midway, a first-person fighting game that invites players to 'finish off' their opponents in spectacularly gory and bloody ways. Most recently, critics have suggested strong links between the hyper-realistic violence in the first-person shooter franchises *Call of Duty* and *Medal of Honor* and violent crime. The anxiety is reminiscent of another medium newly available in our homes in the 1980s. For the first time, movies could be owned and watched at home in video tape format. No responsible cinema owner, box office assistant or movie usher stood between explicit films and the viewing public. There was a noisy public debate about the availability of certain titles, particularly to children. A UK voluntary body, the National Viewers' and Listeners' Association, campaigned to get a series of titles, so-called 'video nasties', censored or banned by the British Board of Film Censors. Over 70 films, including *Cannibal Apocalypse*, *I Spit on Your Grave* and *The Driller Killer*, were prosecuted, around half of them successfully. At the height of the furore in the winter of 1983, the House of Lords debated the link between violent crime and video nasties.

Such concerns are understandable, of course. If there *is* a link between violent video games and violence in the real world, it should be of utmost concern. According to many, including Christopher J. Ferguson, Associate Professor and Department Chair of Psychology at Stetson University, the research doesn't support such a link, though. Recent published studies, including one of Ferguson's own, found no long-term link between violent video games and youth aggression. The most comprehensive study of US high school shootings, conducted by the US Secret Service and the Department of Education and published in the *Journal of Investigative Psychology and Offender Profiling*, concluded that only 15 per cent of perpetrators showed any interest in violent games. The consumption of video games, including violent ones, has increased dramatically since the start of the 1990s, yet violent crime in Europe, the USA, Canada and Australia has decreased equally dramatically over the same period. Rather than society going to hell in handcart fuelled by VHS video tapes and cinema-quality video game warfare, it's enjoying the lowest rates of violent crime since records began.

Intellectual Decline

The other major concern is that video games are making children intellectually lazy. In December 2006, British politician Boris Johnson used his column in

The Telegraph to warn the nation that video games were a cause of ignorance and underachievement. He wrote of video gamers: 'They become like blinking lizards, motionless, absorbed, only the twitching of their hands showing they are still conscious. These machines teach them nothing. They stimulate no ratiocination, discovery or feat of memory.'

In his book *Fun Inc.*, Tom Chatfield draws a parallel between Johnson's concerns and another philosopher, Plato, who wrote:

> *The specific which you have discovered is an aid not to memory, but to reminiscence, and you give your disciples not truth, but only the semblance of truth; they will be hearers of many things and will have learned nothing; they will appear to be omniscient and will generally know nothing; they will be tiresome company, having the show of wisdom without the reality.*

Both authors are concerned that new media are inferior to preceding forms. Johnson points out that video games are a distraction from the written word, whilst the character of Socrates in Plato's *Phaedrus* explains why the written word is dangerously inferior to the practice of spoken debate in 370 BC. Computer and video games, we tell ourselves, will usher in a new era of short attention spans and educational deficit. At the very least, they're bad for our eyesight – right? Again, the research doesn't suggest any such thing.

It's Bad for Your Eyes

Daphne Bavelier has spent more than 25 years studying cognitive neuroscience. She and her laboratory at the University of Geneva, Switzerland study the effect of action video games on the brain and learning.

Her journey into this field was a story of unintended consequences. It started during her postdoctoral fellowship at the Salk Institute in San Diego, where she originally became interested in brain plasticity. Bavelier was fascinated by how the brain adapts, including how it reacts to the removal of one of the senses – for example, deafness. Some time later, when she moved to Rochester University, she began investigating 'useful fields of view' – the visual area over which information can be extracted at a brief glance. She was intrigued by whether this differed in deaf individuals, since previous research documented enhanced peripheral visual attention following early-onset deafness. At the same time, Bavelier was working with a young undergraduate lab tech,

Shawn Green, who piloted the study on himself and a few other students. All the subjects scored near 100 per cent. This was completely unexpected, and far exceeded what was anticipated based on previous studies. They reviewed their findings, checked for errors, and eventually looked for commonalities between the pilot subjects to see if this explained their outlier cohort. What they found was that all of them belonged to an action video game club. The discovery was intriguing – irresistibly so. They changed the project from studying deafness to studying the effect of video games.

A short time later, Shawn Green, who is now on the faculty at the University of Wisconsin, and Bavelier authored a *Nature* article showing that action video games improved attention. Since then, Professor Bavelier's lab has produced seminal papers, including several published in *Nature*, showing that playing first-person point-action video games improves perception, attention, cognition, and in contrast to what parents may tell their children, vision.

Super-happy

Whilst the formative years of video games have been characterised by concerns that they're making us anti-social, lazy and unthinking, there's been a quiet revolution of games that are having a wholly more positive impact on society, and not just in terms of healthy eating and physical fitness. Jane McGonigal, author of *Reality is Broken*, is the designer of the self-improvement game *SuperBetter*, which is all about building resilience. According to McGonigal, study after study has shown that when we're resilient, our body is better able to deal with stress, heal itself and apply the mental focus and determination needed for personal success. The game promotes mental, emotional, physical and social improvements. *SuperBetter* targets the whole person, focusing on energy levels, anxiety and depression, as well as healthy eating and physical fitness. A PowerPack – a package of suggested activities, designed by doctors and researchers at Stanford University, UC Berkeley and Ardmore Institute of Health – contains specific tasks in the form of quests to improve happiness, reduce stress, increase willpower and enhance personal relationships. Activities such as doing something kind for yourself ('I Heart Myself') or making conversation whilst walking your dog ('Human Tagging') build up into a programme of positively reinforced actions and awards.

This is a really surprising development in the field of video games. It would take a full tank of fuel in a car taken without the Liberty City owner's consent to arrive at this point. We're about as far removed from unrelenting tabloid and pressure group criticism as we can be. *SuperBetter* is a video game, of sorts, that claims to help with depression. Whilst there are a range of treatments for depression, many who need help don't get it because therapies can be expensive and, in many cultures, highly stigmatised. Here, as a result of the high availability of smartphones and broadband Internet, is a resource that's extremely low-cost. If it works, then the benefit to society is significant. And there's evidence that it does work. In March 2014, Anne Marie Roepke of the University of Pennsylvania published the results of a trial that demonstrated reduced levels of anxiety and stress as a result of participation in *SuperBetter*. The study was a randomised trial using three control groups: one that used a version of *SuperBetter* based on cognitive behavioural therapy, a second that used positive, feelgood activities, and a third that were put on a waiting list. After one month, there were measurable improvements in anxiety, self-efficacy, satisfaction and social support in those who had used *SuperBetter*.

Dr Martin Seligman, Professor of Psychology at the University of Pennsylvania and author of *Flourish: A Visionary New Understanding of Happiness and Well-being*, is endeavouring to update our understanding of happiness. As the co-founder of the field of positive psychology, he has identified five elements to human happiness: *positive emotions, engagement, relationships, meaning and purpose,* and *achievement*. Seligman advocates positive action, or tuning our happiness. The way we think and act, particularly about the future, shapes our present and ongoing state of mind. Simply put, what we do can make us happy.

McGonigal built *SuperBetter* on many of these principles. She argues that depression can be characterised as a pessimistic view of our own capabilities and a despondent lack of energy, and that games are the exact opposite. Games are engaging – the right game for the right person, highly so. Some will quickly tire of *Call of Duty* warfare, but may have to exercise extreme self-control to not play yet another level of *Candy Crush Saga*. Games are also optimistic demonstrations of our own capabilities. Gamers spend most of their time failing – as much as 80 per cent, according to some studies – yet they continue. That level, boss, puzzle or platform will be defeated providing the player has 'one more go'.

Super-social

The early days of gaming may or may not have been dominated by young, single males fuelled by energy drinks and pizza. The reality today, though, defies the stereotypes. In the report *Essential Facts About the Computer and*

Video Game Industry, the Entertainment Software Association concludes that 'People of all ages play video games. There is no longer a stereotype game player, but instead a game player could be your grandparent, your boss, or even your professor.'

The gender balance is almost even: male players make up 52 per cent, while 48 per cent are female. The number of female gamers aged 50 years or older increased by almost a third between 2012 and 2013, and the majority of gamers play with friends, family members, parents or their spouse. In fact, the top three reasons why parents play games with their children include the fact that it's an ideal opportunity for parents and children to socialise.

More than half of all games played today are played socially. Sixty-five per cent of games are played with others in the same room or online with people they know.

Mission Roundup

The game *Red Dead Redemption* from Rockstar Games, the publishers of *Grand Theft Auto*, contains a lot of violence. There are consequences, though. Shooting citizens at random results in a decrease in honour and an increase in the bounty on your head. The reverse is also true. Helping a woman in distress increases your ranking, and you may be financially rewarded. Most violent games, like other forms of media, apply a moral context. Like all social influences, video games can be neutral, bad, good or all of these. Games, though, engender cohesion over corrosion. People like each other more when they've played games together. Golfers swap friendly taunts about handicaps, five-a-side footballers indulge in (mostly) good-natured trash talk, and video gamers likewise swap barbs before, during and after intense sessions of competitive play.

Any shared game involves social commitment. We agree to turn up, even if virtually, at a mutually convenient time. We agree to play by the same rules, share a code of conduct, make a social commitment and be sensitive to the enjoyment of others. Each shared game, win or lose, is an opportunity to develop social bonds. Games provide an opportunity to exercise the universal human need to relate to, connect with and interact with others.

PART III
Designing for People

Chapter 12

Engagement Loops

The Game

Charles 'Chuck' Coonradt was stuck for words. He knew, as a consultant, that he was supposed to have all the answers, and at this moment he most certainly did not. He was visiting a factory that made prefabricated homes on a production line. He was observing the process from a second-floor window with the plant manager, a man in his mid-50s, who had just given Coonradt what Coonradt himself called the 'kids today' lecture. When the manager had finished painting a sepia picture of his own generational values and work ethic, he pointed to the factory floor below and asked Coonradt: 'What are you going to do about that?' Coonradt observed eight twenty-somethings working on a production line at a pace that he would later characterise as 'arthritic snails in wet cement'. Before Coonradt answered – or, more accurately, didn't answer – he was saved by the bell. A clanging announced lunchtime, at which point the eight men dropped their hammers, picked up a basketball, ran 50 yards down the factory floor and played 42 minutes of feverishly paced basketball. Coonradt considered the level of frenetic energy being expended, turned to the plant manager, and said: 'I don't think you have a raw material problem.'

The Badges

- Gamification Granddaddy

- Feedback Fiend

- Loop-de-loop

- Self-improver

The Grandfather of Gamification

Coonradt founded his business, The Game of Work, in the 1970s. He was driven by national pride and a belief in human nature. He refused to accept the notion that US workers were any less efficient than any other in an increasingly globalised economy. He knew that there was a reason, beyond the obvious, why people seemingly working harder at recreation than the job they were being paid for. Decades before anyone had used the term 'gamification' and when video gaming was little more than *Pong*, he launched a business dedicated to understanding and applying 'the motivation of recreation'. The stark contrast between a spirited game of basketball and lethargic labour troubled him, to the extent that he dedicated his career to the notion that people will pay for the privilege of working harder rather than working when they get paid. Today, he's referred to as 'the grandfather of gamification' by, amongst others, *Forbes* contributor Ken Krogue.

In their book *The Game of Work*, Coonradt and Lee Nelson identify five key factors that perpetuate our enthusiasm for leisure activities:

1.   feedback

2.   score-keeping

3.   goals

4.   coaching

5.   choice.

These all exist in our work life. Businesses set objectives, keep score, train and coach. Even the issue of choice is not intractable. We've already seen that to work is as natural as resting, and that in the right circumstances we will readily choose *grinding* over *goofing off*. When it comes to leisure activities, though, these factors are just better designed to connect with us and motivate us. As an example, let's look at the first item in Coonradt's list: feedback.

Feedback

We receive feedback constantly. We know whether we're driving within a speed limit because a speedometer, often the largest and most prominent gauge on a car dashboard, tells us. Cars, or at least their navigation systems, also tell us whether we're going to make an appointment based on our estimated time of arrival and the speed at which we're travelling. Many will adjust the information based on real-time traffic and road conditions. We determine whether we're losing weight by regularly standing on bathroom scales. We're given feedback in the workplace too, perhaps in an annual appraisal process where busy managers try to distil a full 12 months' worth of feedback in one sitting. Indeed, the widespread practice of annual appraisals is our first clue as to why feedback in the workplace is less effective than that on the field, court, screen or game board.

We adjust what we do, the speed at which we drive, the route we take, the way we conduct ourselves, based on feedback. We see this in leisure, work, in fact all aspects of our lives. We might spend less based on an unhealthy current account balance, or more if buoyed up by a recent interest or bonus payment. It isn't just feedback from gauges and screens, of course. A common source of feedback is other people. Our relationships with partners, family and colleagues are a rich source of sometimes welcome, sometimes unwelcome insights into our own behaviours.

Human feedback can be highly subjective. We may feel it unfair, tainted by history, emotions or office politics. In contrast, the weighing scale, bank statement or medical check-up holds no grudge or misguided sense of loyalty. It neither wants to encourage or discourage. Its feedback is objectively black-and-white and accurate to two decimal places. Neither are perfectly in tune with our behaviour, though. We can save later, drink less tomorrow, exercise at the weekend. This, along with our tendency to imperfect and selective recall, can dilute the impact of even the best feedback. We can pile on weight in spite of regularly stepping on the scales, and have too little sleep in spite of having a clock in each room of our home. It's pointless to try to calculate the impact of that five-kilometre run, a day of calorie counting or the damage done by a chocolate eclair by standing on the scales at the end of the day. Our bodies are not so simple that we can understand the impact of a day's worth of behaviour. It's not uncommon for those on a diet to hop on the scales several times a day – sometimes after each meal. It's feedback, but not at a level of granularity that we can easily and readily use to make choices in the moment. Naturally, those with an eye for the longer term are looking for patterns, not an instant reading. Determination, willpower and commitment usually push us past imperfect guidance. Nevertheless, there's growing evidence that improving feedback can bring about widespread and predictable personal change. The lifestyle of individuals and the behaviour of communities can be improved not by education, not by coercion, but by providing highly contextualised insight. Well-designed feedback can be a potent force for change, and is a cornerstone of gamification, in the form of the *feedback loop*.

Feedback Loops

According to Thomas Goetz, writer and co-founder of health technology business Iodine, a feedback loop involves four distinct stages. The first is the *evidence* stage, which involves measuring, capturing and storing data. The second is the *relevance* stage, where data must become emotionally resonant with us, because its raw form rarely represents sufficient context for us to internalise it. Once we've made a connection with the evidence, we must be able to see a clear path ahead. This is the *consequence* stage. Finally, the fourth stage is *action*. There must be a clear moment when we alter course, recalibrate our behaviour, make a choice, and act. This new action is then measured, and the feedback loop repeats, each action stimulating new insights and altered behaviours that move us closer to our goals.

Figure 12.1   Feedback loop

In Ford's hybrid cars, the instrument cluster includes a graphic display to help measure the energy used when accelerating. The display is a representation of a vine. Efficient driving is rewarded with more vines and more leaves. Energy usage is captured as *evidence*, the representation of a vine makes the evidence *relevant* to drivers sensitive to the ecological impact of driving, its growth or decline is the *consequence*, and mindful driving, characterised as 'hypermiling', is the *action*. Blooming vines and leaves provide an emotionally powerful feedback loop, at once similar and very different to a speedometer.

From dashboard visualisations, we can move to one of a growing number of personal life-monitoring mobile apps, *UP Caffeine* from wearable technology firm Jawbone. With a couple of taps, a pleasantly coloured blue bottle fills with brown caffeine drops for each cappuccino, americano or flat white the user records. The brown droplets move a needle slowly from 'Calm' to 'Wired', and the time required for the effects to dissipate sufficiently for a restful night's sleep increases. Evidence is gathered with each cup of coffee, it's displayed in a highly relevant way, with departing from a state of calmness the consequence to help users make long-term changes to their caffeine intake. Caffeine droplets and vine leaves are feedback loops designed to provoke a visceral and emotional response that results in behavioural change far more effectively than a simple number, gauge, bar or pie chart.

Loop Timing

The four stages of feedback loops describe the process, the step-by-step connection between feedback and behavioural change. Implicit in these steps are two properties which make them effective, two properties often missing from established, traditional feedback mechanisms: *timing* and *visibility*.

PERFECTLY TIMED

If a speedometer only calculated our highest, lowest and average speed at the end of each journey, we'd probably pick up a few speeding tickets. To influence our driving behaviour, the feedback must be instant. This isn't to say that instant feedback is always better than delayed and summarised feedback. Faster isn't necessarily better. Rather, the cadence of the feedback must match the cadence of the change.

Bill Murray is responsible for one of the best-known military cadence calls. In the film *Stripes*, he and fellow recruits, including the late John Candy, march to their version of the song 'Doo Wah Diddy'. Actual cadence calls, such as 'The Duckworth Chant', which includes a call of 'sound off' and a response of 'one-two' and 'three-four', set a marching cadence of 120 beats per minute, whilst others set a running cadence of 180 beats per minute. Cadence calls keep everyone marching in perfect time, and like many military terms, 'cadence' has made its way into the business lexicon to describe management cycles. Cadence is a feedback loop.

Management cycles are typically, but not always, monthly, quarterly and annually. Retail and other fast-moving businesses may meet daily to review feedback and adjust plans accordingly. Many, though, meet monthly to review the performance of the preceding month, in order to adjust plans and activities for the coming month. The more strategic the meeting, the more forward-looking the planning needs to be, and usually the more senior the management involvement. During this form of feedback loop, information is reviewed using business intelligence or analytic applications. Reports, charts and dashboards keep everyone informed of business fundamentals such as revenue, profitability and the quantity of products manufactured or sitting on a shelf. Decisions are made as part of cadence, but rarely executed. This requires tasks and activities to be rolled down to individual contributors, so our feedback loop is fractured. A decision is made at one level, according to one cadence, but action is taken at another. To meet the demands of an organisation, each objective must be cascaded down to a level meaningful to the team or individual, and the timing must align at each stage. A corporate buyer must make daily decisions that impact costs and quality which are assessed by a management team monthly. A marketing campaign decided upon today must be planned, communicated and will become a reality task-by-task, meeting-by-meeting. Corporate health, like our personal well-being, is the result of many smaller decisions. Ross Smith, Microsoft's Director of Testing and a gamification pioneer, in an interview for the *American Journal of Play*, identifies that gamers naturally seek this feedback, that they 'canvass the surrounding environment for hints on how to improve'. Gamified feedback loops provide positive reinforcement for short-term goals, keeping everyone on track for longer-term ones.

VISIBLE

Dan Hill is a London-based designer and blogger. His career has been focused on integrating design, technology and people. Whilst at the BBC, Hill and his team played a pivotal role in reimagining the organisation for the on-demand age. They introduced *iPlayer*, podcasting and any number of groundbreaking digital initiatives. Latterly, Hill has chosen to turn his eye for design on urban innovation as an Executive Director for Future Cities Catapult. Here, Hill is evolving a vision that includes real-time dashboards for buildings, neighbourhoods and cities. Hill, in his blog *City of Sound*, describes the notion as 'a system that makes previously invisible aspects of people's behaviour visible'. This is a succinct characterisation of what well-designed digital feedback loops are capable of. In Hill's own words, they can 'change individual and collective behaviour'. In a digital world, we can all assess the impact of turning the thermostat up or down, we can all check whether a glass of fruit juice counts towards our five (or seven) a day, but few do so at the moment they make the decision. Insight is invisible – at least at the point when it's needed. Hill brilliantly summarises this. By making previously invisible aspects of our life visible, we reconnect behaviour and consequence into a feedback loop.

ACTIONABLE

For feedback to work, it must take the form of a timely, clear and uninterrupted loop between the insight and the action it informs. It must be easy to relate to the behaviour we want to influence in a continuous feedback loop.

Quantified Self

The notion of systems that make visible things that are invisible, or at least opaque, is being increasingly applied to ourselves. It can be surprisingly difficult to understand the root cause of our own personal energy levels. Feeling energised or tired could be related to sleeping habits or altered caffeine intake. It could also be that our energy levels today are as a result, good or bad, of a change in eating habits over the preceding days. Our *joie* or *mal de vivre* may have nothing to do with sleep patterns or food – it might be the consequence of the state of our family or professional life. Unresolved relationship issues can be draining, whilst the unconditional support of a loved one can boost morale. Even though we know ourselves the best, it can be difficult to know for sure what's behind our general state of mind or health, let alone the steps we need to take to improve them. Whilst we increasingly look to changes in lifestyle over medication to improve our health, it can be difficult to know, beyond the very broadest of advice, what specific changes we need to make. General guidance to cut down on dairy or wheat products may or may not be good advice, but without feedback loops, it's difficult to connect directly to a difference in well-being days or weeks later.

Thomas Christiansen is co-founder of Mymee, a health coaching business that changes behaviour through technology and data. Christiansen describes himself as a self-tracker – he knows how many times he has sneezed since 2011. He plots his diet, sleep and travel too, not out of idle curiosity, but to better understand his allergies. Steep upticks in a cumulative graph of sneeze volume signal the onset of pollen seasons. Comparing pollen seasons and dietary information, he was able to determine the impact of gluten and dairy on the intensity of his symptoms and adjust his diet to manage and control them. Christiansen is an advocate of the Quantified Self movement, an international collaboration of users who use or make tracking tools. Quantified Self Labs is a California-based company founded by *Wired* magazine editors and technology thought leaders Gary Wolf and Kevin Kelly that organises meetings, conferences, expositions, forums, content and services to support self-trackers – individuals who want to derive meaning from their personal data.

Mission Roundup

The impact of feedback on human behaviour has been explored for decades, most notably by Stanford psychologist Albert Bandura in the 1960s. In his paper 'Cultivating Competence, Self-Efficacy and Intrinsic Interest through Proximal Self-motivation', Bandura observed that giving individuals a clear goal and a means to evaluate their progress towards it increased the likelihood that they would achieve it.

Gamified feedback loops have been borrowed, as a term, from other fields such as biology and control systems. They are commonplace in the military, in athletic clubs and in engineering. The continuous cycle of evidence–relevance–consequence–action is a powerful motivator when well designed and timely.

Evidence, in the form of data, is becoming easier and easier to collect with digital systems. The iPhone 6 added a barometer to the three-axis gyro, accelerometer, proximity sensor and ambient light sensor built into previous models. Now that we are inseparable from our mobile devices, every movement and moment is capturable as data. Online systems allow each click, page view and social interaction to be recorded and analysed, often in real time. Well-designed systems can make this evidence meaningful, along with virtual representations of what are often physical consequences, so that the next positive action is inevitable.

Business systems have this same opportunity. Traditional processes in complex businesses provide feedback, but in ways that are often disconnected from outcomes. The evidence doesn't resonate, the consequences aren't obvious, the actions are unclear. Poor feedback loops disconnect the action from the result, and impede our understanding and motivation. Well-designed feedback loops let us know when we've hit a milestone or accomplished a goal, and encourage the next positive action. This is the key to understanding, to resonance, to change and to human engagement.

Chapter 13
The Purposeful Play Design Process

The Game

Video games have produced many iconic characters. Perhaps you recall the cartoon blundering of Dirk the Daring from the 1980s arcade game *Dragon's Lair* or the euphemistically named and scythe waving Horned Reaper from the 1990s console game *Dungeon Keeper*. Uniquely, the character Vault Boy from the *Fallout* series is neither playable nor a character in the series, and yet his golden hair, beaming smile and thumbs-up stance is instantly recognisable to anyone who has played the post-apocalyptic franchise. Even those who don't play games will be aware of *Halo*'s Master Chief or *Tomb Raider*'s Lara Croft. To video game fans, one such icon is Duke Nukem. He's a swaggering, testosterone-fuelled hero inspired by 1980s action heroes. *Duke Nukem 3D* sold over 3 million copies, became one of the top-selling video titles ever, and it left fans delirious for a sequel. Fast-forward to 2011, and the sequel *Duke Nukem Forever* was released. Its development had been troubled, with previews and release dates rescheduled many times. As a result of poor sales, publisher Take-Two was forced to reduce its profit estimates, and gamer sites named *Duke Nukem Forever* the most disappointing game of the year.

Duke Nukem Forever had many advantages. It was widely anticipated by its own market, helmed by the co-founders of 3D Realms, the creators of the original version, and extremely well-funded. Technically, it contained many of the elements we've covered in previous chapters. It taps into our intrinsic motivations, it has an engaging narrative, and the sense of progress is well-paced. Nevertheless, by any reasonable measurement, as a game, it failed on release. If not all games are successful – and this is manifestly the case – then why would we think that adding game elements to workplace applications would guarantee their success? What is it that will make your gamification initiative successful?

The Badges

- Business Analyst

- Purposeful Designer

- Completionist

- Walkthrough Expert

The Purposeful Play Design Process

This is where we take all the concepts we've explored and use them as tools to design a gamified experience. Gamification present tremendous opportunities to the modern, agile enterprise. It's a nascent discipline, so applying a structured process will help avoid some of those mistakes that stem from enthusiasm rather than thoughtfulness and preparedness. The tools are powerful, so it's understandable that we may want to apply them quickly without necessarily applying too many rules. After all, isn't a gamified experience supposed to be about emotion, play and fun?

One of the underlying principles of gamification is that it's driven by information and metrics. That, at its rock-solid foundations, is data. This is true, of course, but far too many traditional systems projects stall at this stage, as a measured amount of investigation and debate develops into full-blown *analysis paralysis*. Don't let your gamified initiative fall into this trap either.

What's required is a design framework that takes the best of contemporary and agile systems development and the principles that have been proven in the field of game design to bridge the gap – an approach that's neither too playful nor overly analytical. What follows is the Purposeful Play Design Process, or PPDP. The name is designed to be both analytical, because systems designers love an acronym, but it's actually pronounced playfully as a single four-syllable word: Pee-Pee-Dee-Pee.

The Principles of Pee-Pee-Dee-Pee

Before outlining the PPDP steps, we should remind ourselves of some of the core principles behind the approach. No set of steps, tasks, activities or actions is enough by itself. It should be supported by an understanding of the mindset required to apply the steps – the principles of the Purposeful Play Design Process, Pee-Pee-Pee-Dee-Pee, if you will.

THE HUMAN DESIGN PRINCIPLE

Traditional software design, as we've explored in previous chapters, is focused on systems of transaction and record. It largely ignores the individual who will use the software with nary a passing glance in the form of user experience design. Instead, PPDP requires *design thinking* – an approach to solving design problems by understanding user needs and building insights to solve those needs. It requires not just a functional understanding of the user, but empathy built up through observation and understanding.

THE PURPOSE PRINCIPLE

The overriding principle of PPDP is that *purpose.* Your initiative should be grounded in the purpose of the business, and your business should be grounded in purpose. Many organisations have a vision statement. However, most, but not all, are insipid, generic and uninspiring. One exception is Southwest Airlines. It announced a new vision in 2014: 'to become the world's most loved, most flown, and most profitable airline'. Whilst this is ambitious, even inspiring, now consider its purpose: 'to connect people to what's important in their lives through friendly, reliable, and low-cost air travel'. The difference is that purpose is more human. Businesses need to make a profit – this is how they survive – but we can connect with the Southwest purpose because tells a story about its impact on people.

THE GAME ELEMENTS PRINCIPLE

There's some disagreement about the definition of game mechanics. For example, game designer and author Raph Koster makes his views clear in his blog post 'Narrative Is Not a Game Mechanic'. A contrary view is easy to find. Mattie Brice, a reviewer and writer for the blogs *Moving Pixels*, *The Border House* and *GameCritics*, argues exactly the opposite. To Brice, game mechanics are all about the experience they create for players, such as fun and anxiety. If this is the case, Brice argues, that narrative is a game mechanic, and game mechanics can also be narrative elements.

Kevin Werbach, Wharton Professor and co-author with Dan Hunter of *For the Win*, has devised a framework of game elements that comprises dynamics, mechanics and components. Dynamics are the highest level, and include constraints and emotions, whilst mechanics are the elements that drive the game forward, such as challenges, chance, rewards and turns. Finally, components such as badges, leaderboards and levels are the most specific.

More broadly, though, mechanics, dynamics and components can be thought of as *game elements* – as the basic building blocks of games. They are abstracted when discussing gamification far more often than the subject of pure game design, because gamification is not about building a game. Instead, it's concerned with integrating game mechanics into a non-gaming system. It's embedding game elements into activities that are not, in themselves games. Leave the definition of game mechanics to game designers. Rather than get distracted about defining what a game mechanic is or isn't, look for inspirations in games, and take these inspirations as elements into your gamification initiative.

THE KILLER QUESTION PRINCIPLE

For a significant portion of my career, I've managed teams of people that are responsible for developing software. Each new engineer was educated in the programming languages, tools and databases they needed to build applications. Modern rapid and agile development approaches require software engineers, designers and business people to work closely together, so they were also coached in consulting craft skills, such as active listening, dealing with conflicting requirements and expectation management.

They were also coached in an approach we termed 'the killer question'. Requirements for, say, a management dashboard would be challenged with the question, 'When you have that information, what do you do with it?' It was a reality check, designed to tie the requirement to business need. It freed the designer to think about many possible options rather than being limited by whatever solution was in mind or in place today. We had a dozen variations of killer questions, and whilst this was no more than 'advanced common sense', it often resulted in creative alternatives that surpassed expectations. It's a principle of understanding, for each requirement, why it's needed, and what difference it will make to the business.

THE INTRINSICITY PRINCIPLE

Human motivation is complex. A change of job title to vice president or director might be about status for some and personal growth for others. Making quota for sales reps, in my experience, is not just about the cash.

An engaging design will have considered the four key intrinsic motivators:

1.   **Mastery** – I want to get better at what I do.

2.   **Autonomy** – I want a degree of control on how I do it.

3.   **Purpose** – I want what I do to make a difference in the world

4.   **Social or relatedness** – I want to connect with my colleagues, customers and community.

THE SANDBOX PRINCIPLE

The design of a gamified initiative should include choice. There may be multiple ways of earning points, even though they all serve a common business outcome. There should also be a variety of challenges, more than one win state, and they should be built around a number of motivations. There should also be ways to customise the experience for the individual. For example, *SuperBetter* includes the ability to build quests that are unique to the individual. Any element that customises the experience is an input to the overall sense of autonomy.

Again, we're designing for people. Whilst we generalise that sales professionals are all competitive, marketers creative and finance team members analytical problem-solvers, the reality is that there are always differences.

The PPDP Steps

With the principles of human design, purpose, game elements, killer questions, intrinsicity and sandbox in mind, it's time to follow five key design steps.

STEP 1: DESIGN FOR THE BUSINESS

This step is closest to traditional systems design, but, as is consistent with agile development approaches, documentation is kept to a minimum. A significant proportion of my career has been spent working with businesses to help them build software solutions, and this step is critically important. Firstly, define the business outcome intended to be served by the gamification initiative. Whilst the temptation is to specify vague outcomes, such as 'improve employee engagement', 'drive adoption of the new CRM system' or 'increase team collaboration', business outcomes should be tied to specific and measurable objectives. These might include:

- Reduce staff attrition by 5 per cent year on year.

- Maintain the number of cases raised by supported customers in line with the prior year whilst increasing the number of supported customers by 7 per cent.

- Improve the Net Promoter Score such that there are more promoters than detractors by the end of the financial year.

- Win 10 new, large enterprise customers (new logos) over the next six financial quarters.

- Increase usage of the new system from 62 per cent adoption in any one calendar month to 75 per cent.

- Increase data quality (specifically, the absence of previously missing fields) by 25 per cent.

STEP 2: DESIGN FOR THE PLAYERS

The users or players of enterprise gamification will typically be customers, employees or a social community. Here the word 'social' isn't intended in the sense of non-work-related activity, instead it describes a human group with a common interest – in the case of *Zamzee*, they're children leading an overly sedentary lifestyle; with Nike+, they're customers; in the case of the *SuMo* app, they're employees, and with *Artesian*, they're very specifically sales professionals.

Design thinking requires spending time with players. The questions are a mix of traditional systems design methods, such as asking for the steps an employee goes through to perform their job. It also includes questions that would be absolutely overlooked when designing systems of record – and that's rather the point. These would include what they like and dislike, what tasks they find rewarding and which ones they don't. If the player's a customer, then understand what they value, why they're buying your services or products rather than those of a competitor, and ask for suggestions about what can be improved. In all cases, look for motivations that are aligned with your business objective.

Build player personas

Here we're borrowing from the toolbox of professional marketers, who routinely build *buyer personas*. They're interested in gender, age, profession, financial situation, purpose, shopping habits and so on.

Player personas go beyond the player types suggested by Bartle or Kim, both of whom were designing for games rather than gamified systems, but they're great references when thinking about player personality types. Like buyer personas, they should include gender and age, but they should also include roles, responsibilities, a typical day in their lives, personality types, motivations, objectives, how they behave in terms of the business activity before the application of gamification, and how they're expected to behave once it's implemented.

Finally, identify the players' *goals*.

Design player interaction

It's commonly assumed that we all react well to competition – an assumption that's almost always carried into the first attempt at any gamified design initiative. Of course, this is not true. A deeper understanding of the business objective and players and their personal details will provide the answers, but consider collaborative as well as competitive elements. An initiative to ensure that standards of ethics are understood across the organisation doesn't need winners, losers and leaderboards.

There may also be very little player interaction if the experience is intended to be solo rather than multiplayer. A growing number gamified initiatives fall under the Quantified Self movement, and are focused on self-improvement rather than competition or status.

STEP 3: DESIGN THE EXPERIENCE

Experience platform

We should start with the simplest step, by determining which digital platform or platforms the initiative will be implemented on. Selecting the online and mobile environments is a big decision. The more platforms, the greater the costs, so this choice will undoubtedly be constrained. Consider the following options:

- web (and on which browsers?);

- mobile (iOS, Android, Windows, BlackBerry?);

- wearables (proprietary, such as Jawbone UP and Apple Watch, or open platforms, such as Pebble).

Experience narrative

This step aligns the objective of the business with the player experience. The story should be fun and inspiring. It might include elements of theming which provide input into the design of many of the other elements, including icons, badges, challenges and level names.

The narrative will describe progression through the gamified initiative and where the business objectives and player goals overlap. It doesn't matter if there are non-overlapping goals, providing the narrative can include sufficient commonality on which to design the initiative.

The narrative will also identify what elements of fun are to be included. Again, we're designing for gamification rather than video games, but inspiration can be found in Nicole Lazzaro's 4 Keys 2 Fun, including curiosity, surprise, wonder, excitement and achievement.

Experience elements

Remember that we're not designing a game, instead we're designing an experience that includes game elements. *SuperBetter* includes quests, power-ups and achievements, but it's not a game. Rather, it's a self-improvement application that's highly engaging as a result of integrating game elements.

There are many game mechanics to choose from, and the initiative will benefit from considering those other than points, badges and leaderboards. Not all game mechanics will work in a gamified initiative. The following list includes those mechanics that have successfully made the transition from games to gamification:

- **Points** (*Mastery*) – Points are used to provide feedback and reinforce positive activity.

- **Challenges** (*Purpose, Mastery*) – The ultimate outcome of a gamified initiative is an achieved objective. It's one long quest, divided into smaller ones to maintain a sense of progress.

- **Badges** (*Mastery, Social*) – These are a creative expression of challenges achieved and an indication of social reputation.

- **Levels** (*Mastery, Purpose*) – These provide longer-term feedback on progress and incremental difficulty.

- **Community** (*Social*) – Collaborating and working with others towards common goals or quests.

- **Leaderboards** (*Mastery, Social*) – These typically generate competition, allowing benchmarking of personal progress against that of others.

Experience loops

Well-designed feedback is a primary characteristic of gamified experiences. The player should have a real sense of progress through activities that are a balance of challenge and achievability.

The design considerations are as follows:

- **Evidence** – What activity needs to be measured and what data captured?

- **Relevance** – How will the player experience the feedback, what will make it resonate emotionally?

- **Consequence** – What options will the player have, based on the feedback?

- **Action** – How will the player choose to interact with the gamified experience?

Evidence in gamification, as in life, should be grounded in data. If the objective is to reduce customer services call waiting times, then historical information is needed, along with an understanding of how it's going to be captured and stored for the duration of the initiative.

Experience progression

Whilst experience loops provide quality feedback and stimulate one form of motivation, experience progression is required to provide a sense of development, growth and mastery.

The initiative should provide a sense of escalating difficulty as the player progresses. In massively multiplayer online role-playing games such as *World of Warcraft*, moving from Level 1 to Level 2 takes less time than moving from Level 29 to Level 30. A gamified initiative that rewards players for contributing to support forums might award the status of Junior Contributor for five posts, Senior for 10, but Principal status might require 20 or more.

STEP 4: DESIGN THE ECONOMY

Gamified experiences have an economy. Loyalty programmes usually reward customer choice with discounts. The *Artesian* Social Seller score rewards customer-focused activity with points that build reputation in the form of social capital. The social network score Klout rewards shared expertise with a number that represents influence.

Brian Burke, in his book *Gamify: How Gamification Motivates People To Do Extraordinary Things*, identifies four types of game economy:

1. **Fun** – discovery, delight, excitement;

2. **Self-esteem** – recognition, progress, mastery, praise;

3. **Social Capital** – connections, likes, status, friends, helpfulness;

4. **Things** – cash, rewards, discounts, points.

The player economy should also consider time:

- **Duration** – How long will the initiative run?

- **Frequency** – How often will the economy calculate the results – daily, weekly, monthly?

- **Metrics** – What data from which systems is required to support the initiative and measure its success?

- **Currency** – What is the point system, and how does it support experience loops and progression?

STEP 5: MEASURE, ITERATE AND REFINE

Design is an iterative process, and one that benefits from experience and input. Website designers routinely use something called 'bivariate testing', where two versions of the website exist simultaneously, but with subtle differences. Text reassuring customers that their payments are secure might accompany each product description on one version, and sit alongside the shopping cart on another. It might simply involve two different colour palettes. In any case, after a short period of testing, the more successful version is taken forward, with two new variations. Bivariate testing assumes that some things work better than others. It's an approach that doesn't get hung up on failure; instead, it tests what works, adjusts, and moves forward with more tests.

Mission Roundup

Following the PPDP will provide you the space to design for aligning business objectives and player enjoyment. It will offer an opportunity to model a gamified initiative prior to its being built, so that you can identify and address challenges. Wrinkles can be ironed out before the development team starts its work.

However, be flexible though as the design becomes reality. Some things work well in principle, but not in practice, so be pragmatic as the vision becomes real. Apply the principles, follow the process, be flexible and agile, and your gamified initiative will have the best possible chance of success in bringing about the transformational change you promised your business.

The Walkthrough

Video game walkthroughs are instructional videos, images and text that help new players, or players who are stuck, through some of the challenges others have already conquered. What follows is a gamification walkthrough – chocolate-coated balls of wisdom that have been generously shared by those who've already experienced success in designing and developing their own gamification initiatives, including the iBehave and London Gamifiers communities and the team from CloudApps:

1.   **Focus** – It's tempting to address all of the organisation's behavioural change and engagement issues whilst you have the gamification toolbox open and the budget approved, but resist doing this. Instead, focus on one to five key behaviours, or fewer for a first initiative.

2.   **Mundanification** – Trying to make mundane tasks more engaging through gamification is rarely successful. Instead of gamification, consider revisiting the business process to identify whether the task could be automated, mitigated, minimised or eliminated. There are greater opportunities for the business than this.

3.   **Settling** – Leaderboards mean winners, losers and a vast expanse of middle ground. This presents many challenges, not least that those people in the middle ground can begin to settle. They're not going to win, nor are they going to be singled out for being last, so they may be tempted to coast through the initiative. To avoid settling, build two or three leaderboards. These can be based on behaviour (challenges) time (weekly, monthly, all-time), teams or peer groups.

4.   **Endless** – Gamification is a process rather than a one-off project. However, each initiative should be kept short, perhaps thirty days or less, in order to maintain a sense of the immediate and to keep interest levels high. Whilst there are certainly many successful quarterly initiatives, they're probably on the margins of gamification.

5.   **A moment to learn** – The easier the initiative is to understand, the better. Make sure that the first achievements are related to getting started with the initiative, so that there's an early sense of achievement and reward.

6.   **A lifetime to master** – Well, perhaps not a lifetime, but a sense of increasing achievement is accomplished by increasing the difficulty as the gamification initiative progresses. The rate at which points, badges and achievements are won should slow down as the initiative progresses.

Chapter 14

Afterword

Those of you who have arrived at this point via the previous chapters are living proof that, in spite of living with information 'hyperabundance', we're still capable of engaging in long-form argument. There are those, like Nicholas Carr, author of *The Shallows: How the Internet is Changing the Way We Think, Read and Remember*, who will be delighted that you have practised the ancient art of 'deep reading'. I stand right beside them as they shake your hands and thank you for joining us. I trust the trip has been worthwhile, without too many diversions or wrong turns. *World of Workcraft* though is not a destination, it is a waypoint. As we continue to innovate with digital motivation we will discover more about the field and about ourselves.

Clifford Stoll is the author of a surprisingly thrilling non-fiction book, *The Cuckoo's Egg*, in which, in attempting to resolve a rounding error on the university's computers, he detects and eventually hunts down a West German hacker who is selling information to the KGB. Stoll is also a brilliant scientist. Even the great and the good are capable of getting it wrong, though. In an infamous article in *Newsweek* (originally titled 'The Internet? Bah! Hype Alert: Why Cyberspace Isn't, and Will Never Be, Nirvana', but now titled 'Why the Web Won't Be Nirvana'), Stoll argued that predictions of electronic commerce, telecommuting, virtual classrooms and online communities were 'baloney'. To be fair, the article was written in 1995, and it can take nothing away from Stoll's brilliance. However, time has proven Stoll not just to be wrong on this occasion, but exactly wrong. Retail, learning and business systems have been and continue to be utterly transformed by the Internet.

Marc Andreessen, entrepreneur, software engineer and one of the creators of the Web browser *Mosaic*, proclaimed that software was 'eating the world' in a well-known editorial in the *Wall Street Journal*. At that time, in 2011, he noted the disruption that businesses such as Amazon and Netflix were causing. High streets around the world have been transformed by online retailing, but software hasn't stopped consuming traditional business thinking. Hospitality will never be the same again thanks to Airbnb, and once someone has used

Uber, their expectations of taxi services have changed forever. It isn't difficult to see that every industry, high technology or otherwise, will ultimately be transformed by the application of mobile, cloud and social technologies.

Etsy.com is a rapidly growing marketplace famous for vintage and handmade items. It also deploys more than 30 software updates each and every day. Software giant Microsoft achieved desktop dominance by providing upgrades to its *Office* suite every two years. Cloud software giant Salesforce updates three times a year. Likewise, subscribers to *Office 365*, the online cloud version of Microsoft's productivity software will see major updates quarterly. This just isn't fast enough for Etsy, as much experts in agile management practices and continuous software delivery as they are in retro retailing.

Industries comprise businesses, businesses comprise people. They are social constructs comprising individuals organised around a common purpose, albeit an economic one. Organisation theorist Russell Ackoff wrote in his 1993 paper *From Mechanistic to Social Systemic Thinking* of three ages of the corporation. The first was the *mechanistic*, as characterised by Ford and the production line. The second was the *biological*, as suggested by twenty-first-century human resource and management practices, where a department leader is likely to be a 'head' rather than a 'controller' – people have heads, they're not machines. The third age, though, according to Ackoff, would be *social*. The parts of a social corporation each have their own purpose, which must be served if the corporation is to be served.

And software is no longer exclusive to corporate budgets. In fact, individuals are bringing their own technology to the workplace as part of a groundswell movement referred to as Bring Your Own App (BYOA) or Bring Your Own Device (BYOD). Chief information officers are no longer completely in control of the technology that runs their organisation.

Software, then, is also becoming more social, more personal, more human. This represents an opportunity to reinvent work: replacing inflexible process with agile and continuous improvements, eliminating tedious tasks and re-engaging individuals in challenging, meaningful work. Business has been utterly transformed by the Internet. Now, it's the turn of our social interactions: the way we relate with one another, and the way we relate to ourselves. As it nears ubiquity, there is no corner of the human condition that is unreachable by technology.

References

Accel-Team. 'Employee Motivation: Theory and Practice'. *Accel-Team*, 2015. Web. 8 Feb. 2015.

Accenture. *Connecting the Dots on Sales Performance*. Accenture, 2012. Web. 8 Feb. 2015.

Ackoff, Russell. 'OSU Libraries.' *From Mechanistic to Social Systemic Thinking: Russell L. Ackoff*. OSU Libraries, 18 Jan. 1994. Web. 29 Mar. 2015.

Adkins, Amy. 'Majority of U.S. Employees Not Engaged Despite Gains in 2014'. *Majority of U.S. Employees Not Engaged Despite Gains in 2014*. Gallup, 2014. Web. 26 Mar. 2015.

Amabile, Teresa. *Creativity in Context*. Boulder, CO: Westview, 1996. Print.

Amabile, Teresa, and Steven Kramer. *The Progress Principle: Using Small Wins to Ignite Joy, Engagement, and Creativity at Work*. Boston, MA: Harvard Business Review Press, 2011. Print.

Amabile, Teresa, William Dejong and Mark R. Lepper. 'Effects of Externally Imposed Deadlines on Subsequent Intrinsic Motivation'. *Journal of Personality and Social Psychology* 34.1 (1976): 92–8. Web. 8 Feb. 2015.

Amano, Takashi, and Cliff Edwards. 'Nintendo Seen Missing Target as Sony-Microsoft Dwarf Wii U'. *Businessweek*, 3 Dec. 2013. Web. 8 Sept. 2014.

Andreessen, Marc. 'Why Software Is Eating The World'. *Wall Street Journal*, 20 Aug. 2011. Web. 29 Mar. 2015.

Angelos, Jason, and Mark Wachter. *Boosting the Effectiveness of Sales Compensation*. Society for Human Resource Management, 2 June 2013. Web. 31 Aug. 2014.

'Apple's Market Value Hits $600bn'. *BBC News*, 4 Oct. 2012. Web. 5 Sept. 2014.

Ariely, Dan. *Predictably Irrational: The Hidden Forces that Shape Our Decisions*. New York: HarperCollins, 2008. Print.

Ariely, Dan, Uri Gneezy, George Loewenstein, and Nina Mazar. 'Large Stakes and Big Mistakes'. *Review of Economic Studies* 76.2 (2009): 451–69. Web.

Ariely, Dan. *The Upside of Irrationality: The Unexpected Benefits of Defying Logic*. New York: Harper Perennial, 2010.

Ariely, Dan. *The (Honest) Truth about Dishonesty: How We Lie to Everyone – Especially Ourselves*. New York: HarperCollins, 2012. Print.

Ariely, Dan, George Loewenstein and Drazen Prelec. 'Tom Sawyer and the Construction of Value'. *Journal of Economic Behavior and Organization* 60 (2006): 1–10. Web. 8 Feb. 2015.

Ariely, Dan. 'What's the Value of a Big Bonus?' *The New York Times*, 19 Nov. 2008. Web. 30 Mar. 2015.

Aron, Jacob. 'Online Petition Stalls Plan to Ban Violent Videogames in Germany'. *The Guardian*, 28 July 2009. Web. 8 Sept. 2014.

AVG. 'Digital Birth: Welcome to the Online World'. *Business Wire*, 6 Oct. 2010. Web. 30 Aug. 2014.

Babauta, Leo. *Zen Habits: Handbook for Life: Hundreds of Tips for Simplicity, Happiness and Productivity*. West Valley City, UT: Walking Lion, 2009. Print.

Baer, Drake. 'Kleiner Perkins Partner Bing Gordon: LinkedIn Is A Game, And Your Job Will Be Gamified'. *Fast Company*, 31 July 2013. Web. 27 Mar. 2015.

Baker, Bruce. 'Digital Homo Economicus'. *The Center for Integrity in Business*, Seattle Pacific University, 28 June 2012. Web. 30 Aug. 2014.

Baker, Chris. 'Will Wright Wants to Make a Game Out of Life Itself'. *Wired*, 23 July 2012. Web. 8 Sept. 2014.

Ballve, Marcelo. 'Wearable Computing Goes Mainstream – Consumers are Already Snapping Up Smart Watches and Wristbands'. *Business Insider*, 8 Aug. 2013. Web. 31 Aug. 2014.

Bandura, Albert, and Dale H. Schunk. 'Cultivating Competence, Self-efficacy, and Intrinsic Interest through Proximal Self-motivation'. *Journal of Personality and Social Psychology* 41.3 (1981): 586–98. Web.

Bartle, Richard. 'Hearts, Clubs, Diamonds, Spades: Players Who Suit MUDs'. *mud.co.uk*, 28 Aug. 2014. Web. 30 Aug. 2014.

Bartle, Richard. 'Bartle Test of Gamer Psychology'. *GamerDNA*, n.d. Web. 26 Mar. 2015.

Bavelier, Daphne, and Richard J. Davidson. 'Brain Training: Games to Do You Good'. *Nature*, 28 Feb. 2013. Web.

Beck, Kent et al. *Manifesto for Agile Software Development*, 2001. Web. 30 Aug. 2014.

Betters, Elyse. 'Space Invaders: Blast from the Past that Still Inspires'. *BBC News*, 30 May 2013. Web. 5 Sept. 2014.

Bishop, Todd. 'Xbox 360 vs. Wii vs. PS3: Who Won the Console Wars?' *GeekWire*, 2 Aug. 2013. Web. 8 Sept. 2014.

Blythe, Mark A. *Funology: From Usability to Enjoyment*. Dordrecht: Kluwer Academic, 2003. Print.

Bradshaw, Tim. 'Nike's FuelBand Runs into Trouble – FT.com'. *Financial Times*, 21 Apr. 2014. Web. 22 Mar. 2015.

Brice, Mattie. 'Narrative Is a Game Mechanic'. *Moving Pixels*, 31 Jan. 2012. Web.

Brown, Gardner M., and Jason F. Shogren. 'Economics of the Endangered Species Act'. *Journal of Economic Perspectives* 12.3 (1998): 3–20. Web. 8 Feb. 2015.

Brown, Tim. *Change by Design: How Design Thinking Transforms Organizations and Inspires Innovation*. New York: HarperBusiness, 2009. Print.

references

Burke, Brian. *Gamify: How Gamification Motivates People to Do Extraordinary Things*. Boston, MA: Bibliomotion, 2014. Print.

Burke, Brian. 'Most Gamification Apps Will Fail – Gartner'. *Information Age*, 27 Nov. 2012. Web. 5 Sept. 2014.

Burke, Brian. 'The Gamification of Business'. *Forbes*, 21 Jan. 2013. Web. 5 Sept. 2014.

Burnett, Dean. 'Claims that "Video Games Lead to Violence" Lead to Violence'. *The Guardian*, 20 Sept. 2013. Web. 8 Sept. 2014.

Carr, Austin. 'Nike: The No. 1 Most Innovative Company of 2013'. *Fast Company*, 11 Feb. 2013. Web. 21 Mar. 2015.

Carr, David F. 'Kaplan Expands Gamification of Online Courses'. *InformationWeek*, 27 June 2013. Web. 7 Sept. 2014.

Carr, Nicholas. *The Shallows: How the Internet is Changing the Way We Think, Read and Remember*. London: Atlantic Books, 2011. Print.

Carse, James. *Finite and Infinite Games*. New York: Free Press, 2013. Print.

Chakrabortty, Aditya. 'Why We Buy What We Buy'. *The Guardian*, 20 May 2008. Web. 24 Mar. 2015.

Chatfield, Tom. 'Can Video Games Alter Society in a Good Way?' *The Huffington Post*, 6 Sept. 2013. Web. 8 Sept. 2014.

Chatfield, Tom. *Fun Inc.: Why Gaming Will Dominate the Twenty-first Century*. New York: Pegasus, 2010. Print.

Chen, Liyan. 'The World's Biggest Public Companies'. *Forbes*, 5 July 2014. Web. 5 Sept. 2014.

Chou, Yu-kai. *Yukai Chou Gamification*. Web. 8 Feb. 2015.

Cichelli, David. *Compensating the Sales Force*. New York: McGraw-Hill, 2004. Print.

Cichelli, David. '2013 Sales Compensation Practices Survey to Reveal Program Management Trends'. *David Cichelli Blog and Videos*, 17 Aug. 2013. Web. 31 Aug. 2014.

Cichelli, David. 'Sales Compensation Trends: 2012 Survey Results'. WorldatWorkTV, *YouTube*, 23 Jan. 2012. Web. 31 Aug. 2014.

Cleaver, Sean. 'Storytelling 117 – The Successful Narrative Evolution of Halo'. *Stuff & Nonsense: Sean Cleaver*, 16 Dec. 2012. Web. 8 Sept. 2014.

Coonradt, Charles A., and Lee Nelson. *The Game of Work: How to Enjoy Work as Much as Play*. Salt Lake City, UT: Shadow Mountain, 1984. Print.

Covert, Bryce. 'This Company Has a 4-Day Work Week, Pays its Workers a Full Salary and is Super Successful'. *ThinkProgress*, 18 Apr. 2014. Web. 27 Mar. 2015.

Covey, Steven. *The 7 Habits of Highly Effective People*. New York: Free Press, 1989. Print.

Csíkszentmihályi, Mihály. *Flow: The Psychology of Optimal Experience*. New York: Harper Perennial, 1991. Print.

Dane, Patrick. 'Inside the Gaming Studio: Halo 4's Narrative Director Armando Troisi'. *WhatCulture*, 6 Nov. 2012. Web. 8 Sept. 2014.

Dauenhauer, Bernard. 'Paul Ricoeur'. *Stanford Encyclopedia of Philosophy*, 11 Nov. 2002, rev. 18 Apr. 2011. Web. 8 Sept. 2014.

Deci, Edward L. 'Effects of Externally Mediated Rewards on Intrinsic Motivation'. *Journal of Personality and Social Psychology* 18.1 (1971): 105–15. Web.

DelVecchio, Susan, and Judy Wagner. 'Motivation and Monetary Incentives: A Closer Look'. *Journal of Management and Marketing Research* 7.1 (2011): 1–13. Web. 8 Feb 2015.

Denning, Steve. 'The Future Workplace is Now: How Etsy Makes 30 Innovations per Day'. *Forbes*, 4 Apr. 2014. Web. 20 Sept. 2014.

Denning, Steve. 'Why Software is Eating the World'. *Forbes*, 11 Apr. 2014. Web. 20 Sept. 2014.

Deterding, Sebastian. 'Meaningful Play: Getting Gamification Right'. *GoogleTechTalks*, 24 Jan. 2011. Web. 31 Aug. 2014.

Deterding, Sebastian. 'Meaningful Play: Getting Gamification Right'. *Slideshare*, 31 Jan. 2011. Web. 8 Sept. 2014.

Diaz, Anne-Christine. 'Behind the Work: Volkswagen's "The Fun Theory"'. *AdvertisingAge*, 7 Oct. 2009. Web. 30 Aug. 2014.

Dicken, Kent. 'Why Southwest Uses a North Star to Navigate'. *Shared IDiz*, 6 Aug. 2013. Web. 8 Sept. 2014.

Drucker, Peter. *The End of the Economic Man: A Study of the New Totalitarianism*. London: Heinemann, 1939. Print.

Drucker, Peter. *The Landmarks of Tomorrow*. New York: Harper, 1959. Print.

Dryden, Jane. 'Autonomy'. *Internet Encyclopaedia of Philosophy*. Web. 8 Sept. 2014.

Duhigg, Charles. *The Power of Habit: Why We Do What We Do, and How to Change*. New York: Random House, 2013. Print.

Dunn, Mary Elizabeth. 'The Effect of Narrative Elements within Video Games: Localized Setting and Character Motivation on Audience Arousal'. Thesis, University of Texas at Austin, 2012. Web. 8 Feb. 2015.

Earle Mcleod, Lisa. 'How P&G, Southwest, And Google Learned To Sell With Noble Purpose'. *Fast Company*, 29 Nov. 2012. Web. 29 Mar. 2015.

Edmondson, Amy C. 'Strategies for Learning from Failure'. *Harvard Business Review*, Apr. 2011. Web. 14 Sept. 2014.

Edwards, Benj. 'Ten Things Everyone Should Know about Space Invaders'. *Vintage Computing and Gaming*, 26 June 2008. Web. 5 Sept. 2014.

Edwards, Tom. *iMedia Connection Blog*. Web. 8 Feb. 2015.

Elgan, Mike. 'The Joy of Glogging'. *Computerworld*, 27 July 2013. Web. 31 Aug. 2014.

Elgan, Mike. 'What Wearable Computing is Really All About'. *Computerworld*, 17 Aug. 2013. Web. 31 Aug. 2014.

Entertainment Software Association. *Essential Facts About the Computer and Video Game Industry*. ESA, 2014. Web. 8 Feb. 2015.

Erickson, J. 'Agile Software Development, and Extreme Programming'. *Journal of Database Management* 16.4 (2005): 88–100. Web. 8 Feb. 2015.

Evans, Benedict. 'Mobile is Eating the World'. *Slideshare*, 17 May 2013. Web. 30 Aug. 2014.

Fahlman, Garin. 'Talking Transmedia, Writing & Halo 4 with Armando Troisi'. *Vancouver Weekly*, 9 Apr. 2013. Web. 8 Sept. 2014.

Feldman, Jonathan. 'SXSW: What Gaming Should Teach IT Leaders'. *InformationWeek*, 3 Oct. 2012. Web. 21 Sept. 2014.

Ferguson, Christopher J. 'The School Shooting/Violent Video Game Link: Causal Relationship or Moral Panic?' *Journal of Investigative Psychology and Offender Profiling* 5.1–2 (2008): 25–37. Web.

Ferguson, Christopher J. 'Video Games Don't Make Kids Violent'. *Time*, 7 Dec. 2011. Web. 8 Sept. 2014.

Fierlinger, Philip. 'Agile, Blasphemy & Burning Bridges – UX Design Day'. *Xero Blog*, 17 Oct. 2013. Web. 20 Sept. 2014.

Fogg, B.J. 'A Behavior Model for Persuasive Design'. *Proceedings of the 4th International Conference on Persuasive Technology*. New York: ACM, 2009. Print.

Fredheim, Helge. 'Why User Experience Cannot Be Designed'. *Smashing Magazine*, 15 Mar. 2011. Web. 13 Sept. 2014.

Frey, Bruno S. *Not Just for the Money: An Economic Theory of Personal Motivation*. Cheltenham: Edward Elgar, 1997. Print.

Gallo, Carmine. 'Southwest Airlines Motivates its Employees with a Purpose Bigger than a Paycheck'. *Forbes*, 21 Jan. 2014. Web. 7 Sept. 2014.

Galloway, Paul. 'Video Games: Seven More Building Blocks in MoMA's Collection'. *InsideOut*, 28 June 2013. Web. 5 Sept. 2014.

'Game Design Grad Armando Troisi Talks Narrative Direction on Halo 4'. *VFS Blog*, Vancouver Film School, 6 Nov. 2012. Web. 8 Sept. 2014.

Gamification World Congress. 'Nick Pelling: The Gamification Inception'. *Gamification World Congress 2014*, 9 May 2014. Web. 19 Sept. 2014.

Garratt, Patrick. 'Miyamoto is Developer "Hero", Says Survey'. *VG247*, 15 June 2009. Web. 8 Sept. 2014.

'Gartner Reveals Top Predictions for IT Organizations and Users for 2013 and Beyond'. Gartner, 24 Oct. 2012. Web. 23 Mar. 2015.

'Gartner Says Worldwide PC, Tablet and Mobile Phone Combined Shipments to Reach 2.4 Billion Units in 2013'. Gartner, 4 Apr. 2013. Web. 22 Mar. 2015.

'Gartner Says Worldwide PC Shipments in the Third Quarter of 2014 Declined 0.5 Percent'. Gartner, 8 Oct. 2014. Web. 21 Mar. 2015.

'Gartner Says Worldwide Video Game Market to Total $93 Billion in 2013'. Gartner, 29 Oct. 2013. Web. 19 Mar. 2015.

Gaudiosi, John. 'New Reports Forecast Global Video Game Industry Will Reach $82 Billion by 2017'. *Forbes*, 18 July 2012. Web. 31 Aug. 2014.

Gladwell, Malcolm. *Outliers: The Story of Success*. London: Little, Brown, 2008. Print.

'Global Workforce Study 2014'. *Towers Watson*, Aug. 2014. Web. 26 Mar. 2015.

Gócza, Zoltán, and Kollin, Zoltán. *UX Myths*. Web. 8 Feb. 2015.

Goetz, Thomas. 'Harnessing the Power of Feedback Loops'. *Wired*, 19 June 2011. Web. 14 Sept. 2014.

Goetz, Thomas. 'Wired's Gary Wolf & Kevin Kelly Talk the Quantified Self'. *Wired*, 18 Oct. 2012. Web. 14 Sept. 2014.

Goldman, Seth, and Barry Nalebuff. *Mission in a Bottle: The Honest Guide to Doing Business Differently – and Succeeding*. New York: Crown Business, 2013. Print.

Gordon, Bing. 'Bing Gordon Interview for Coursera'. Interview by Kevin Werbach. *Coursera Gamification*. Penn University, 2013. Web.

Green, Shawn, and Daphne Bavelier. *Nature.com*, 29 May 2003. Web. 29 Mar. 2015.

Greenfield, Adam. *Everyware: The Dawning Age of Ubiquitous Computing*. Berkeley, CA: New Riders, 2006. Print.

Groom, Dean. '8 Ways Minecraft Works on Your Brain'. *Playable*, 3 Feb. 2013. Web. 31 Aug. 2014.

Guzzo, Richard A., Richard D. Jette, and Raymond A. Katzell. 'The Effects of Psychologically Based Intervention Programs on Worker Productivity: A Meta-Analysis'. *Personnel Psychology* 38.2 (1985): 275–91. Web.

Hachman, Mark. 'Gartner May be too Scared to Say it, but the PC is Dead'. *Readwrite*, 5 Apr. 2013. Web. 30 Aug. 2014.

Hachman, Mark. 'Windows 8 Stabs the PC Market in the Gut'. *Readwrite*, 10 Apr. 2013. Web. 31 Aug. 2014.

Hamel, Gary, *What Matters Now: How to Win in a World of Relentless Change, Ferocious Competition, and Unstoppable Innovation*. New York: John Wiley & Sons, 2012. Print.

Hassenzahl, Marc. 'The Effect of Perceived Hedonic Quality on Product Appealingness'. *International Journal of Human-Computer Interaction* 13.4 (2001): 481–99. Web.

Henricks, Mark. 'How to Gamify Your Company'. *OPEN Forum*, 10 Mar. 2012. Web. 27 Mar. 2015.

Henry, Alan. 'In Defense of Video Games: More than Just an Entertaining Time Sink'. *Lifehacker*, 2 Jan. 2012. Web. 8 Sept. 2014.

Henry, Alan. 'SuperBetter is a Game that Rewards You for Healthy Living and Working Towards Your Goals'. *Lifehacker*, 17 Apr. 2012. Web. 8 Sept. 2014.

Hewitt, Chris. '4 Tips for Reducing Stress and Improving Well Being: Mindbloom's Chris Hewett Shares Insights'. *Tech Cocktail*, 10 June 2012. Web. 31 Aug. 2014.

Hicks, Jon. 'How the Xbox 360 Won the Console War'. *TechRadar*, 6 Nov. 2013. Web. 8 Sept. 2014.

Hill, Dan. 'Sketchbook: The Personal Well-Tempered Environment'. *Cityofsound*, 2008. Web. 29 Mar. 2015.

Hoggins, Tom. 'Can the Next Generation Revitalise the Console Industry?' *The Telegraph*, 27 Nov. 2013. Web. 8 Sept. 2014.

'Homo Economicus?' *The Economist*, 7 Apr. 2005. Web. 30 Aug. 2014.

'HSBC Removes Sales Incentives for Staff'. *Which?*, 20 Feb. 2013. Web. 31 Aug. 2014.

Irlenbusch, Bernd. 'When Performance-related Pay Backfires'. *LSE*, 2009. Web. 30 Mar. 2015.

Isaac, Mike. 'Jawbone Unveils "Up", a Health Monitoring Wristband for Data Fiends'. *Wired UK*, 3 Nov. 2011. Web. 31 Aug. 2014.

Johnson, Boris. 'The Writing is on the Wall – Computer Games Rot the Brain'. *The Telegraph*, 28 Dec. 2006. Web. 8 Sept. 2014.

Johnson, Bradford C., James M. Manyika and Lareina A. Yee. 'The Next Revolution in Interactions'. *McKinsey Quarterly*, Nov. 2005. Web. 31 Aug. 2014.

Jones, Huw. 'UK Banks Agree to Pay for Latest Mis-selling Scandal'. *Reuters*, 22 Aug. 2013. Web. 31 Aug. 2014.

Kahneman, Daniel, and Amos Tversky. 'Choices, Values, and Frames'. *American Psychologist* 39.4 (1984): 341–50. Web.

Kamal, Ashok. 'Green Gamification: The Apps, Sites, and People that are Going to Save Our Planet'. *VentureBeat*, 30 Jan. 2013. Web. 30 Aug. 2014.

Kapko, Matt. 'How Gamification Drives Business Objectives'. *CIO Magazine*, 28 May 2014. Web. 29 Mar. 2015.

Karafezov, Petar. 'Learning Can be Fun and Rewarding – Learn with LevelUp for Photoshop'. *Petar Karafezov*, 7 Nov. 2011. Web. 6 Sept. 2014.

Keen, Cathy, and Erin Fluegge Woolf. 'Fun at Work Makes it Easier for Employees to Function on the Job'. *University of Florida News*, 17 July 2008. Web. 4 Sept. 2014.

Kim, Amy Jo. 'Gamification 101: Design the Player Journey'. *Slideshare*, 26 Jan. 2011. Web. 5 Sept. 2014.

Kim, Amy Jo. 'Social Engagement: Who's Playing? How Do they Like to Engage?' *Amy Jo Kim*, 19 Sept. 2012. Web. 30 Aug. 2014.

Klein, Sarah. '4 Science-backed Ways to Motivate Yourself to Work Out'. *The Huffington Post*, 5 Sept. 2014. Web. 5 Sept. 2014.

Knaack, Jay A. *Rational Self-interest*. New York: Graduate School of Arts and Science, New York University, 1973. Print.

Kober, Jeff. 'Disney Service Basics'. *MousePlanet*, 29 Nov. 2007. Web. 8 Feb. 2015.

Kober, Jeff. *The Wonderful World of Customer Service at Disney* Kissimmee, FL: Performance Journeys Publishing, 2009. Print.

Kohn, Alfie. *Punished by Rewards: The Trouble with Gold Stars, Incentive Plans, A's, Praise, and Other Bribes*. Boston, MA: Houghton Mifflin, 1993. Print.

Koster, Ralph. 'Narrative Is Not a Game Mechanic'. *Raph Koster's Website*, 20 Jan. 2012. Web. 29 Mar. 2015.

Krogue, Ken. '5 Gamification Rules from the Grandfather of Gamification'. *Forbes*, 19 Sept. 2012. Web. 8 Sept. 2014.

Krogue, Ken. *Ken Krogue*. Web. 8 Feb. 2015.

Kuittinen, Tero. 'Nintendo Loses Grip on Home Console Market'. *Forbes*, 8 May 2013. Web. 8 Sept. 2014.

Kushner, David. 'The Guitar Heroes'. *Upstart Business Journal*, 17 Sept. 2007. Web. 31 Aug. 2014.

Lahey, Jesse. 'Improving Life, One Game at a Time'. Audio blog post. *Engaging Leader*, 6 Sept. 2013. Web. 6 May 2015.

Lammie, Rob. 'From Ant to City and Beyond: A History of All Things Sim'. *Mental Floss*, 30 Jan. 2013. Web. 8 Sept. 2014.

Lang, Harris A., B. Oates and K. Seau. 'Systems Analysis and Design: An Essential Part of IS Education'. *Journal of Information Systems Education* 17 (2000): 241–8. Web. 31 Aug. 2014.

Lazzaro, Nicole. 'The 4 Keys 2 Fun'. *XEODesign*. Web. 8 Feb. 2015.

Lazzaro, Nicole. 'Why We Play Games: Four Keys to More Emotion Without Story'. Oakland, CA: XEODesign, 8 Mar. 2004. Web. 8 Feb. 2015.

Lazzaro, Nicole. '4 Keys To Fun'. Lecture by Nicole Lazzaro. California College of the Arts, Timken Lecture Hall, San Francisco Campus, San Francisco. 24 Mar. 2015. Lecture.

'Lords Debate Violent Crime and Video Nasties'. British Universities Film & Video Council, 16 Nov. 1983. Web. 8 Sept. 2014.

Lowe, Dylan. 'Meet the Man Who Measures Everything'. *Business Insider*, 23 Apr. 2012. Web. 14 Sept. 2014.

Manjoo, Farhad. 'High Definition: The "Gamification" of the Office Approaches'. *The Wall Street Journal*, 12 Jan. 2014. Web. 5 Sept. 2014.

Marczewski, Andrzej. 'Bartle's Killers: A Misunderstood Group of People'. *Gamified UK*, 24 June 2013. Web. 30 Aug. 2014.

Marczewski, Andrzej. 'Extrinsically and Intrinsically Motivated User Types'. *Gamified UK*, 8 July 2013. Web. 31 Aug. 2014.

Marshall, John, and Matthew Adamic. 'The Story is the Message: Shaping Corporate Culture'. *Journal of Business Strategy* 31.2 (2010): 18–23. Web. 8 Feb. 2015.

Martin, Rebecca. 'World of Warcraft Boosts Users Social Skills: Swedish Study'. *The Local se*, 21 Apr. 2011. Web. 30 Aug. 2014.

Mayerowitz, Scott. 'Frequent Flier VIP: Meet the Guy Who Never Waits at the Airport'. *ABC News*, 17 Dec. 2009. Web. 30 Aug. 2014.

McLeod, Lisa Earle. *Selling with Noble Purpose: How to Drive Revenue and Do Work that Makes You Proud*. Hoboken, NJ: Wiley, 2012. Print.

McGonigal, Jane. 'Gaming Can Make a Better World'. *TED Talks*, Feb. 2010. Web. 8 Feb. 2015.

McGonigal, Jane. *Reality is Broken: Why Games Make Us Better and How They Can Change the World*. London: Vintage, 2012. Print.

McGregor, Douglas. *The Human Side of Enterprise*. New York, McGraw-Hill, 1960. Print.

Metz, Rachel. 'A Wearable Computer More Powerful than Glass, and Even More Awkward'. *Business Insider*, 27 Aug. 2013. Web. 31 Aug. 2014.

Mill, John Stuart. 'Essay V: On the Definition of Political Economy; and on the Method of Investigation Proper To It' (1844). *Essays on Some Unsettled Questions of Political Economy. Library of Economics and Liberty*. Web. 30 Aug. 2014.

Mill, John Stuart. *On the Logic of the Moral Sciences: A System of Logic (1856)*. London: Routledge/Thoemmes, 1997. Print.

Murakami, Haruki, and Philip Gabriel. *What I Talk about When I Talk about Running: A Memoir*. New York: Alfred A. Knopf, 2008. Print.

O*Net OnLine. 'Summary Report for: 27-2012.01 – Producers'. *O*Net OnLine*, 2011. Web. 30 Aug. 2014.

Orland, Kyle. 'Activision: Over 20 Million Black Ops Players Log More than 600 Million Hours'. *Gamasutra*, 28 Dec. 2010. Web. 30 Aug. 2014.

Overfelt, Maggie. 'How "Horrendous Failure" Led to Rock Band'. *CNNMoney*, 3 Sept. 2009. Web. 31 Aug. 2014.

Oxlade, Andrew. 'HSBC is Latest Bank to Axe Staff Sales Targets'. *The Telegraph*, 20 Feb. 2013. Web. 31 Aug. 2014.

Paharia, Rajat. *Loyalty 3.0: How to Revolutionize Customer and Employee Engagement with Big Data and Gamification*. New York: McGraw-Hill, 2013. Print.

Parsons, Tom. 'Southwest Celebrating 40 Years of Flights'. *The Dallas Morning News*, 7 June 2011. Web. 8 Sept. 2014.

Perman, Stacy. 'For Some, Paying Sales Commissions No Longer Makes Sense'. *The New York Times*, 20 Nov. 2013. Web. 11 Sept. 2014.

Pink, Daniel H. 'A Radical Prescription for Sales'. *Harvard Business Review*, Aug. 2012. Web. 31 Aug. 2014.

Pink, Daniel H. *Drive: The Surprising Truth about What Motivates Us*. Edinburgh: Canongate, 2011. Print.

Pink, Daniel H. *To Sell is Human: The Surprising Truth about Moving Others*. New York: Riverhead, 2012. Print.

Poundstone, William. *Priceless: The Hidden Psychology of Value*. London: Oneworld Publications, 2011. Print.

Prashant, John. 'Enterprise Gamification: Beyond the Badges (and the Hype)'. *Kwench*, 20 May 2013. Web. 7 Sept. 2014.

Priebatsch, Seth. '3 Powerful Game Dynamics that Create Brand Superfans'. *Fast Company*, 17 Nov. 2011. Web. 31 Aug. 2014.

Priebatsch, Seth. 'Welcome to the Decade of Games'. *Harvard Business Review*, 9 Sept. 2010. Web. 31 Aug. 2014.

Public Broadcasting Service. 'Men's Occupations'. *The First Measured Century*. Arlington, VA: PBS. Web. 31 Aug. 2014.

Purde, Andrus. 'We Chatted to Dan Pink, the Author of "To Sell Is Human"'. *Pipedrive Blog*, 2 Dec. 2013. Web. 11 Sept. 2014.

Radhakrishnan, Mohana. 'Game On! How Learning Wins with Gamification'. *Learning in the Cloud*, Nov. 2013. Web. 7 Sept. 2014.

Raphael, Daniel. 'The Impact of Video Games on this Generation'. *The Huffington Post*, 7 Nov. 2013. Web. 8 Sept. 2014.

Reeves, Byron. 'Byron Reeves: What Makes a Game Addictive?' mediaXstanford, *YouTube*, 24 Nov. 2010. Web. 31 Aug. 2014.

Reeves, Byron. 'Games that Change the Nature of Work'. *Slideshare*, 24 June 2012. Web. 5 Sept. 2014.

Reeves, Byron, and J. Leighton Read. *Total Engagement: How Games and Virtual Worlds Are Changing the Way People Work and Businesses Compete*. Boston, MA: Harvard Business School Press, 2009. Print.

Rigby, Scott, and Richard M. Ryan. *Glued to Games: How Video Games Draw Us in and Hold Us Spellbound*. Westport, CT: Praeger, 2010. Print.

Roberts, Dale, and Rooven Pakkiri. *Decision Sourcing: Decision Making for the Agile Social Enterprise*. Farnham: Gower, 2013. Print.

Roberts, Michelle. 'Diets Fail Because Advice is Wrong, Say Researchers'. *BBC News*, 22 Sept. 2011. Web. 14 Sept. 2014.

Roepke, Anne Marie. 'A Randomized Controlled Trial: The Effects of SuperBetter on Depression'. Philadelphia, PA: University of Pennsylvania in Collaboration with SuperBetter Labs, LLC, 2013. Web. 8 Feb. 2015.

Ryan, Marie-Laure. 'From Playfields to Fictional Worlds: A Second Life for Ariosto'. *New Literary History* 40.1 (2009): 159–77. Web. 8 Feb. 2015.

Ryan, Richard M., and Edward L. Deci. 'Intrinsic and Extrinsic Motivations: Classic Definitions and New Directions'. *Contemporary Educational Psychology* 25.1 (2000): 54–67. Web.

Schawbel, Dan. 'Adam Penenberg: How Gamification is Going to Change the Workplace'. *Forbes*, 7 Oct. 2013. Web. 12 Oct. 2013.

Schreier, Jason. 'Sid Meier: The Father of Civilization'. *Kotaku*, 26 June 2013. Web. 8 Sept. 2014.

Schwartz, Barry. *The Paradox of Choice: Why More is Less*. New York: Harper Perennial, 2005. Print.

'Scientist Plays World of Warcraft for 250 Days, Develops Mad Social Skillz'. *news.com.au*, 22 Apr. 2011. Web. 30 Aug. 2014.

Seligman, Martin. *Flourish: A Visionary New Understanding of Happiness and Well-being*. New York: Free Press, 2012. Print.

Shah, Helen, and Emma Dawney. 'Behavioural Economics'. *New Economics*, 22 Sept. 2005. Web. 30 Aug. 2014.

Sharkey, Joe. 'United's Top Flier of 2012 Has Eye on Global Title'. *The New York Times*, 17 Dec. 2012. Web. 30 Aug. 2014.

Sherman, Lawrence. 'Lawrence Sherman at Nudge and Beyond: Behavioural Science, Policy and Knowing What Works'. The British Academy, *YouTube*, 5 Jul. 2012. Web. 30 Aug. 2014.

Shine, Kennedy. 'Why Minecraft Matters'. *Techonomy*, 13 Nov. 2013. Web. 8 Sept. 2014.

Shirky, Clay. 'Clay Shirky's Writings About the Internet'. *Shirky: Situated Software*, 30 Mar. 2004. Web. 31 Aug. 2014.

Shirky, Clay. *Cognitive Surplus: Creativity and Generosity in a Connected Age*. London: Penguin, 2011. Print.

Shirky, Clay. *Here Comes Everybody: The Power of Organizing Without Organizations*. London: Allen Lane, 2008. Print.

Shirky, Clay, and Daniel H. Pink. 'Cognitive Surplus: The Great Spare-time Revolution'. *Wired*, 22 May 2010. Web. 30 Aug. 2014.

Silva, Marlene N. et al. 'Exercise Autonomous Motivation Predicts 3-yr Weight Loss in Women'. *Medicine & Science in Sports & Exercise* 43.4 (2011): 728–37. Web. 8 Feb. 2015.

Sinur, Jim. 'Justifying BPM Projects'. Gartner, 2004. Print.

Smith, Greg. 'Why I Am Leaving Goldman Sachs'. *The New York Times*, 13 Mar. 2012. Web. 29 Mar. 2015.

Smith, Paul. *Lead with a Story: A Guide to Crafting Business Narratives that Captivate, Convince, and Inspire*. New York: Amacom, 2012. Print.

Smith, Ross. 'How Play and Games Transform the Culture of Work'. *American Journal of Play* 5.1 (2012): n.p.

Solis, Brian. 'Blame it On the Youth'. *Brian Solis: Defining The Impact of Technology, Culture and Business*, 27 Apr. 2011. Web. 30 Aug. 2014.

Solis, Brian. *The End of Business As Usual: Rewire the Way You Work to Succeed in the Consumer Revolution*. Hoboken, NJ: Wiley, 2011. Print.

Solis, Brian. *What's the Future of Business? Changing the Way Businesses Create Experiences*. Hoboken, NJ: Wiley, 2013. Print.

Solis, Brian. 'The Conversation Prism'. Brian Solis, 2014. Web.

Spence Jr, Roy M. *It's Not What You Sell, It's What You Stand For*. New York: Portfolio, 2009. Print.

State of the American Workplace 2010–2012. Rep. N.p.: Gallup, n.d. Print.

Steenburgh, Thomas, and Michael Ahearne. 'Motivating Salespeople: What Really Works'. *Harvard Business Review*, Aug. 2012. Web. 31 Aug. 2014.

Stern, Mark Joseph. 'A Little Guilt, a Lot of Energy Savings: How Smiley Faces and Peer Pressure Can Save Money – and the Planet'. *Slate Magazine*, 1 Mar. 2013. Web. 30 Aug. 2014.

Stewart, Bart. 'The Four Bartle Types'. *Gamasutra*, 1 Sept. 2011. Web. 30 Aug. 2014.

Stoll, Clifford. *The Cuckoo's Egg: Tracking a Spy Through the Maze of Computer Espionage*. New York: Pocket Books, 2000. Print.

Stoll, Clifford. 'Why the Web Won't Be Nirvana'. *Newsweek*, 27 Feb. 1995. Web. 8 Feb. 2015.

Strohmeyer, Robert. 'Gamification: Using Play to Motivate Employees and Engage Customers'. *PCWorld*, 28 Aug. 2013. Web. 3 Sept. 2014.

Stuart, Keith. 'SimCity Becomes a World Economy'. *The Guardian Games Blog*, 17 Aug. 2012. Web. 8 Feb. 2015.

Stuart, Keith. 'Violent Video Games, California and the Ambiguity of Freedom'. *The Guardian Games Blog*, 28 June 2011. Web. 8 Sept. 2014.

Suits, Bernard. *The Grasshopper: Games, Life, and Utopia*. Toronto: University of Toronto, 1978. Print.

Sweney, Mark. 'Mars Revives "Work, Rest, Play" Slogan'. *The Guardian*, 28 Feb. 2008. Web. 31 Aug. 2014.

Tarkoff, Rob. 'Choose Customer Service without the Call Centre'. *The Guardian*, 27 Mar. 2013. Web. 30 Aug. 2014.

Thaler, Richard H., and Cass R. Sunstein. *Nudge: Improving Decisions about Health, Wealth, and Happiness*. New Haven, CT: Yale University Press, 2008. Print.

Thompson, Clive. 'Learn to Let Go: How Success Killed Duke Nukem'. *Wired*, 21 Dec. 2009. Web. 6 Sept. 2014.

Underhill, Paco. *Why We Buy: The Science of Shopping*. New York: Simon & Schuster, 2000.

USA. US Secret Service. *The Final Report and Findings of the Safe School Initiative: Implications for the Prevention of School Attacks in the United States*. By Bryan Vossekuil. Washington, D.C.: U.S. Secret Service, 2002. Print.

Van Der Meulen, Rob, and Janessa Rivera. 'Gartner Says Worldwide Video Game Market to Total $93 Billion in 2013'. *Gartner Newsroom*, 29 Oct. 2013. Web. 8 Sept. 2014.

Van Grove, Jennifer. 'Gamification: How Competition is Reinventing Business, Marketing & Everyday Life'. *Mashable*, 28 Jul. 2011. Web. 3 Sept. 2014.

Vedamurthy, Indu, Mor Nahum, Daphne Bavelier, and Dennis M. Levi. 'Mechanisms of Recovery of Visual Function in Adult Amblyopia through a Tailored Action Video Game'. *Nature.com*, 26 Feb. 2015. Web. 29 Mar. 2015.

Ward, Mark. 'Why Minecraft is More than Just Another Video Game'. *BBC News*, 7 Sept. 2013. Web. 8 Sept. 2014.

Wasserman, Elizabeth. 'How to Set Up a Sales Compensation Plan', *Inc.*, 16 Dec. 2009. Web. 31 Aug. 2014.

Weiser, Mark. 'The Computer for the 21st Century'. *Scientific American* 265.3 (1991): 94–104. Web.

Welch, Ned. 'A Marketer's Guide to Behavioral Economics'. *McKinsey Quarterly,* Feb. 2010. Web. 30 Aug. 2014.

Wenning, Todd. 'The Greatest Stocks of the Next Generation'. *The Motley Fool,* 17 Dec. 2009. Web. 8 Feb. 2015.

Werbach, Kevin, and Dan Hunter. *For the Win: How Game Thinking Can Revolutionize Your Business.* Philadelphia, PA: Wharton Digital, 2012. Print.

'What Publishers Need to Know About Gamification'. *Betaout,* 20 Aug. 2013. Web. 5 Sept. 2014.

Wong-Anan, Nopporn. 'Thai Youth Imitates Grand Theft Auto in Cab Murder'. *Reuters UK,* 4 Aug. 2008. Web. 8 Sept. 2014.

Wu, Michael. 'Gamification 101: The Psychology of Motivation'. *Lithium Community,* 3 Jan. 2011. Web. 31 Aug. 2014.

Wu, Michael. 'The Magic Potion of Game Dynamics'. *Lithium Community,* 2 Apr. 2011. Web. 31 Aug. 2014.

YouGov/Cognitomobile Survey Results. Rep. N.p.: YouGov, 2012. Print.

Zichermann, Gabe. 'Byron Reeves – "Games that Change the Nature of Work"'. *Slideshare,* 24 June 2012. Web. 31 Aug. 2014.

Zichermann, Gabe. 'How To: Properly Use Badges to Engage Customers'. *Mashable,* 19 Aug. 2011. Web. 5 Sept. 2014.

Zichermann, Gabe, and Christopher Cunningham. *Gamification by Design: Implementing Game Mechanics in Web and Mobile Apps.* Sebastopol, CA: O'Reilly Media, 2011. Print.

Index

If you have found this book useful you may be interested in other titles from Gower

HyperThinking
Creating a New Mindset for the Age of Networks
Philip Weiss
9781409428459 (paperback)
9781409428466 (e-book – PDF)
9781409484561 (e-book – ePUB)

Managing Innovation Adoption
From Innovation to Implementation
Majharul Talukder
9781472413352 (hardback)
9781472413369 (e-book – PDF)
9781472413376 (e-book – ePUB)

The Out-of-Home Immersive Entertainment Frontier
Expanding Interactive Boundaries in Leisure Facilities
Kevin Williams and Michael Mascioni
9781472426956 (paperback)
9781472426963 (e-book – PDF)
9781472426970 (e-book – ePUB)

Business Transformation Essentials
Case Studies and Articles
Edited by Axel Uhl and Lars Alexander Gollenia
9781472426987 (hardback)
9781472426994 (e-book – PDF)
9781472427007 (e-book – ePUB)

The Digital Renaissance of Work
Delivering Digital Workplaces Fit for the Future
Paul Miller and Elizabeth Marsh
9781472437204 (paperback)
9781472437211 (e-book – PDF)
9781472437228 (e-book – ePUB)

Digital Enterprise Transformation
A Business-Driven Approach to Leveraging Innovative IT
Edited by Axel Uhl and Lars Alexander Gollenia
9781472448545 (hardback)
9781472448552 (e-book – PDF)
9781472448569 (e-book – ePUB)

Decision Sourcing
Decision Making for the Agile Social Enterprise
Dale Roberts and Rooven Pakkiri
9781409442479 (hardback)
9781409442486 (e-book – PDF)
9781409473640 (e-book – ePUB)

Comparative Causal Mapping
The CMAP3 Method
Mauri Laukkanen and Mingde Wang
9781472439932 (hardback)
9781472439949 (e-book – PDF)
9781472439956 (e-book – ePUB)

Visit **www.gowerpublishing.com** and

- search the entire catalogue of Gower books in print
- order titles online at 10% discount
- take advantage of special offers
- sign up for our monthly e-mail update service
- download free sample chapters from all recent titles
- download or order our catalogue